Rethinking Behaviour Management

RESTORATIVE PRACTICES
IN SCHOOLS

Margaret Thorsborne & David Vinegrad

Routledge
Taylor & Francis Group

LONDON AND NEW YORK

Acknowledgements

Many people have helped make this manual a possibility. In particular, we would like to acknowledge the early pioneering work in conferencing by our colleagues in New Zealand, Aotearoa, and later in Australia, when police in New South Wales adapted the "Kiwi" approach to what is now referred to as the "scripted" conference. Many versions of those early manuals have been written by practitioners in a variety of jurisdictions over the ensuing years. It is now timely that a manual be written exclusively for schools, as increasing interest in these approaches has coincided with a need to find more effective ways to manage behaviour in our schools. There is now a critical mass of wisdom to be shared with our education colleagues.

We have been encouraged and assisted in this endeavour by our own colleagues in education across Australia. Isaac Williamson, a delightfully creative conference facilitator and a guidance officer in a busy high school in Queensland, has been an inspiration in this field with his courage and conference wisdom. Margaret Armstrong, an educational advisor and co-manager of the conference pilot in Victorian schools, has been fierce in her advocacy of this process and searched high and low for stories for this manual. They have both given us valuable feedback about its content and design. Donna Brunt, a teacher in a Catholic high school in Victoria, has contributed her adaptations of the restorative theme in ways which we have again found inspirational.

Our partners Mick Brown and Anne Conrick have done the tiresome work of proof-reading and have remained patient as we've toiled away at our computers into the wee hours of the night. They have put up with the erosion of well-earned school vacation time as we've met by plane or long car drive to thrash out the chapters. Edwina Carson, the desktop guru of our first edition, responded cheerfully and with grace to impossible timelines.

Never before in our recent history have we needed so much to build and rebuild relationships so that anger, hatred and violence can be replaced by peace and goodwill. Schools are a great place for this work to be done. This manual will help you to do that.

And finally, we would like to acknowledge those school teachers, welfare staff and administrators, those often unsung heroes, who have instinctively understood what restorative justice has been trying to achieve, and have been doing it anyway.

First published 2002 by Speechmark Publishing Ltd.

Published 2017 by Routledge
2 Park Square, Milton Park, Abingdon, Oxon OX14 4RN
711 Third Avenue, New York, NY 10017, USA

Routledge is an imprint of the Taylor & Francis Group, an informa business

British Library Cataloguing in Publication data
A catalogue record for this book is available from the British Library.

ISBN 9780863886874 (pbk)

Authors:

Margaret Thorsborne   Email: margthorsborne@optusnet.com.au   Web: www.thorsborne.com.au
and David Vinegrad   Email: behaviourmatters@hotmail.com

Illustrations by Adrian Osborne

Previously published in Australia by Inyahead Press.

Contents

Foreword

I have been asked by the authors of this conference facilitator training manual to write a foreword. It is a great pleasure to do so. I have yet to meet David Vinegrad, whom I understand to be a very experienced, creative trainer and facilitator, but I have known Margaret Thorsborne for some years and have long been an admirer of her innovative and pioneering efforts in the introduction of restorative justice techniques into the area of education.

There has been growing international disquiet about the way in which schools manage their internal discipline problems. In many areas and in many countries this has resulted in an increase in suspensions and exclusions of students from school to their and our detriment.

If there is a theme which emerges throughout western communities in the 1990's it has been the theme of "disconnectedness". That has produced a challenge for all of us, particularly those involved in justice systems, to support new initiatives which emphasise the reverse of that and look for reconciliation and positive results from the systems used.

The involvement of community conferencing in school communities has been a remarkable initiative. It is critical that schools take a leading role in crime prevention and in the building of relationships and effective ways of managing behaviour so as to model for their young people a way to deal with these issues constructively in the future.

School conferencing has proven to be highly successful in achieving these purposes. I am convinced that schools play a significant role in teaching young people about their responsibilities and accountabilities to themselves and others. The proof of this is the way in which more and more schools are moving towards this way of working to deal with violations of behaviour in their communities.

What is important is that when this work is done, it is done with a proper acknowledgement of the professional basis and skills involved and is not left to those with good intentions only. It is essential that the work is recognised as requiring a substantial skill and professional base. If this is not done, there is always a risk that greater harm will ensue to the school community and the lessons which are becoming so critical to our communities will be the wrong lessons, not the constructive ones.

Community, family and school conferencing systems are dynamic and ever changing. There are always new challenges, new visions, new energies and new techniques to learn and apply.

This conference training manual will fulfil an important part in keeping up to date with the professional skills required for now – it must however be viewed as a living document which I hope will be added to as new dimensions to this fascinating work are developed.

I commend the manual to all those who wish to contribute to a gentler society.

D J Carruthers
Chief District Court Judge
New Zealand
October, 2002

About this manual

There is no substitute for the learning and engagement that occur when participants take an active part in training role plays or practise conference facilitation in a supportive environment. An essential component of the facilitator training programme is the exchange of ideas and robust debate with workshop leaders and other participants.

We have organised the manual in a way which we hope will be practical and useful to you.

Chapter one begins the analysis of current practice in your school so you can develop some insight into what works and what doesn't and, more importantly, what outcomes the school community seeks to achieve. It offers some compelling arguments about the use of the restorative justice philosophy and practice as an alternative to punishment as a way to manage behaviour.

Chapters two through to seven are devoted to the practice of community conferencing, and are highly practical in their directions, suggestions and tips.

Chapter eight lists some the most frequently asked questions fielded in the training workshops, along with our answers.

The Appendix contains key documents used in the facilitation of the formal conference process, such as the Preparation Checklist, Conference Script and Agreement stencil.

We have also added contributions from a variety of practitioners in the form of case studies, adaptations of the conference process, and 'circles', a traditional approach to problem-solving adapted here for use in classrooms.

There is a list of recommended readings including relevant websites for you to explore further these notions of restorative justice.

We regard this manual as a work in progress. It is designed for ease of change, so please email your feedback, suggestions and questions to us for consideration in later editions.

Good luck!

Margaret Thorsborne and David Vinegrad

We can be reached at: marg@thorsborne.com.au

and

behaviourmatters@hotmail.com

Chapter 1

Restorative justice and behaviour management

Enlightened educational communities are beginning to express concern over the increasing numbers of suspensions and exclusions as schools strive to maintain control over changing populations. Allied agencies such as police and welfare services have concerns that the school system may be contributing to an increase in crime with the use of such sanctions, rather than building a sense of community and citizenship. Research has shown us that the process of alienation and stigmatisation of wrongdoers risks the formation of a subculture within and beyond the school, intent on rejecting the norms of acceptable behaviour as these young people strive to have their needs for belonging and affiliation met. These outcomes, although never intended, work against the promotion of wellbeing, resilience and connectedness in all students. And it may well be that school policy and practice is not taking into account theories of child and adolescent development, or increasing rates of family break-down and community disconnection.

Constructive analysis of discipline/behaviour management policy is clearly warranted, and demonstrates that in most cases, schools have traditionally adopted a quasi-judicial approach to the management of student misconduct, modelled on existing western criminal justice systems. What this means in practice for a school is:

- When codified rules have been broken, sanctions must be applied to the wrongdoers

- There is a belief that discipline= punishment=justice which will change behaviour and achieve compliance

- Punishment is the best form of deterrence and it is important to send a clear and strong message to the school community about what is acceptable and what is not

- The authority of the school has been challenged and control must be restored and maintained

- There is pressure on administrators for a quick fix, so that many suspensions and exclusions are the result of organisational convenience

- That justice is seen to be done through punitive sanctions meted out by administrators often far removed from the incident

- That those affected by the behaviour are excluded from decisions about how to respond

In contrast to these values and attitudes are other school-based endeavours which are about negotiated curriculum and democratic classroom rules, civics and citizenship, emotional competencies, catering to individual student needs, and student-centred classrooms. So, on the one hand, the adults in schools are keen to build relationships with and between students because they are clear about the benefits of this approach for improving learning outcomes. But on the other hand, they risk those very relationships by using punishment in an attempt to change behaviour, when research clearly shows that there are other, more effective ways of doing this.

Those schools that are keen to review their current practice and thinking with a view to reforming policy, and/or are dissatisfied with the outcomes of more traditional approaches, may find the following questions useful to stimulate debate and dialogue:

1. What body of research and evidence supports the school's policies about student behaviour?

2. Who decides what penalties and sanctions are applied to school wrongdoers? How was this decision reached?

3. How does the school justify the use of detentions, suspensions and the exclusion of students?

4. Does the school have different behaviour management procedures for children, adolescents and young adults? Why or why not?

5. How does the school teach emotional intelligence in the curriculum and/or provide conscience-building exercises for wrongdoers?

6. Does the school provide similar levels of professional development for behaviour management as it does for curriculum?

7. What process does the school use to ensure that harmful incidents do not occur again?

8. What process does the school use to ensure collective accountability for harmful behaviour and to establish which parts of the system need to be changed?

9. How are wrongdoers encouraged to take responsibility for their actions? How are they taught to understand the consequences for others of what they have done?

10. How are the needs of victims and their families met by current behaviour management policies?

> *Practitioners in schools have been quick to recognise both the parallels between the justice system and behaviour management and the potential in notions of restorative justice to reform school behaviour management policy and practice.*

Restorative approaches

Just as western criminal justice is being challenged in its failure to curb crime and its increasing prison populations, traditional approaches to behaviour management need to be challenged to cope with increasing levels of family breakdown and community disconnection, the loss of automatic respect for authority, and increasing suspension and exclusion rates. Those attempting to reform our criminal justice systems are moving toward a more restorative approach. Practitioners in schools have been quick to recognise both the parallels between the justice system and behaviour management and the potential in notions of restorative justice to reform school behaviour management policy and practice.

So what do we mean by restorative justice?

Put simply, restorative justice means that:

- Crime (and misconduct) is a fundamental violation of people and interpersonal relationships

- Violations create obligations and liabilities

- Restorative justice seeks to heal and put right the wrongs

(An expansion on these three points can be found in the Recommended Reading section.)

Restorative justice is a participatory and democratic justice that focuses on the community defined by the incident and not just the wrongdoer. It is an approach to harmful behaviour and community conflict that sees wrongdoing as essentially a violation of people and relationships.

The community conference, a well known restorative process, formalises the bringing together of all those responsible for and most affected by wrongful conduct. Individually and collectively people address the causes of the harm and the impact of the harm on those affected, and investigate ways to make amends and minimise the risk of future wrongdoing.

Restorative justice in a school

A 'just' school is a place where victims and wrongdoers and their respective communities of care are active participants in processes that ensure equal justice and fairness. Victims are empowered to have their needs met and to have their experience validated. Wrongdoers are able to tell their stories and given the chance to make amends. And finally, the community of care can seek ways to ensure that the incident does not happen again.

Schools that incorporate principles of restorative justice into student management practices can:

- begin to address the root causes of harmful behaviour rather than reacting to the symptoms
- acknowledge that harm from incidents goes beyond just victims and wrongdoers in the school community
- use restorative practices to address the trauma, repair the harm and reintegrate wrongdoer/s back into the community
- find creative and meaningful ways of responding to violations against people and property and develop preventative strategies
- provide a forum where school community members engage with the wrongdoer/s, administrators are released from the demanding task of 'meting out justice', and schools build significant links with their communities
- bring together the community responsible and accountable for the behaviour, so that resources and knowledge, which would otherwise not be utilised, can be activated
- provide the necessary link between contemporary classrooms and pro-social behaviour management processes across the school
- understand that sometimes a desire for retribution masks a concern for public safety which can be adequately addressed in a restorative way
- make the commitment of time necessary to repairing relationships instead of going down the quick fix path
- "work with" rather than "do to" young wrongdoers.

Restorative practices cannot be viewed as isolated interventions or tools that a school uses only when required. Restorative practices are inextricably linked to all interactions that occur throughout the school day. Clear evidence of a restorative and 'just' school can be seen in the language used, ceremonies conducted, curriculum developed, teacher presentations, student programmes, dialogue in newsletters, the physical environment and 'feel' of the school. In essence, a restorative intervention cannot be an "add-on" to punitive and retributive policy and practices. A school reflecting on how it

manages student behaviour needs to review the complete supportive school environment. Three main areas should be the topic of regular review and the focus for the implementation of restorative practice. These are:

- The provision of programmes that enhance the personal and social competencies of students, teachers and parents, so that daily interactions proceed more positively and generate fewer problems.
- The provision of positive, effective and socially healthy environments for all students.
- The establishment of structures and arrangements so that extra support is available, whenever needed, as an entitlement for all students, and a recognition of the needs of teachers who also need to access sources of support.

Restorative approaches to student management will closely complement 'protective' strategies that schools build into their daily programmes. The capacity of schools to prevent, address and ameliorate negative and harmful behaviours is of prime importance. The 'protective' stages of primary prevention and subsequent successive interventions are ideal foci for the inclusion of restorative and reintegrative approaches to student behaviour.

Are schools already practising restorative justice?

Some schools have been dissatisfied with high numbers of suspensions and exclusions and the frequent use of deterrents such as detentions, conduct cards etc. This has caused a fundamental rethinking of school justice/discipline systems. As a result, they have formulated alternative approaches, many of which have a restorative philosophy embedded in their practice, and have included contemporary research and information about child and adolescent development.

Most schools have insightful practitioners who have been 'doing business' another way for a long time. These classroom teachers incorporate restorative practices on a daily basis in the management of a fair and democratic classroom. As practitioners, they see that relationships are central to managing behaviour and to establishing a supportive environment where the curriculum, behaviour and classroom culture are negotiated and democratic.

Many schools have recognised that a key to a harmonious environment is being able to identify when and how relationships are harmed and to adopt a community wide approach to problem-solving. Protective and preventative programmes currently in schools include (this list is by no means exhaustive):

- Peer Mediation
- Peer Support
- Mental Health Curriculum
- Protective Behaviours
- Responsible Thinking
- Tribes (programme to create a positive school and classroom environment)
- Civics and Citizenship
- Classroom Meetings (often called circles)

These all include some elements that are restorative, place a value on people and relationships and are based on communitarian notions of justice.

The community conference

The community conference, described in detail in this manual, captures the basic philosophy of restorative justice. This manual has been written for schools. The scripted conference, first developed by police in New South Wales, Australia, to divert young wrongdoers away from court, was an adaptation of the Family Group Conference process enshrined in juvenile justice legislation in New Zealand in 1989.

Practitioners in Queensland (Australia) schools in the mid 1990's were quick to see the potential benefits of the process for dealing with serious incidents of misconduct and harm, particularly bullying and violence, and conducted two twelve month pilot programmes to evaluate its effectiveness. Further pilots have been conducted in NSW and Victoria. The evaluations demonstrated that the process had a great deal to offer those schools which valued notions of relationship management rather than more traditional, punitive approaches.

Outcomes included:

- Participants being highly satisfied with the process and its outcomes
- High compliance rate with the terms of the agreement by wrongdoers
- Low rates of repeated wrongdoing
- A majority of wrongdoers felt they were more accepted, cared about and more closely connected to other conference participants following conferencing
- A majority of victims felt safer and more able to manage similar situations than before conferencing
- The majority of conference participantshad closer relationships with other conference participants after conferencing
- All school administrators felt that conferencing reinforced school values
- Most family members expressed positive perceptions of the school and comfort in approaching the school on other matters
- Nearly all schools in the trial reported they had changed their thinking about managing behaviour from a punitive to a more restorative approach

The majority of conferences were in response to assaults and serious victimisation, followed by property damage and theft. Conferences were also used to address incidents involving drugs, damaging the school's reputation, truanting, verbal abuse, persistent disruption in class, and in one case, a bomb threat.

This approach to relationship management has now been adopted by a wide range of schools in many countries, and ongoing research supports the view that the processes and philosophy of restorative justice have enormous benefits for our schools as we strive to develop young people who will make a positive contribution to their communities. ▣

Chapter 2

Decision-making –
to conference or not?

Imagine for a minute that you are the deputy principal on duty, or the head of the middle school, or a student dean. You have just taken a phone call from an anxious parent concerned that their son is refusing to come to school because of some serious bullying that has been happening all term. Or a teacher has just reported a violent assault in the playground during the lunch hour. Or a student might request help to deal with a long running conflict in his or her peer group. Or a group of students has been discovered smoking cannabis behind the gymnasium.

Schools have set policies and procedures which are activated to deal with the immediacy of such incidents: investigating the facts, finding out who has been involved, deciding how to respond. These types of incidents might attract a suspension (or a more permanent sanction) depending on the seriousness, calls home to parents, referrals to the school counsellor. Contacting the police might be required in the case of illicit drug-related incidents. The incident may be so serious in nature (eg sexual assault), that the resolution needs to be decided in another jurisdiction. In this case, premature school involvement in the case may interfere with the judicial process, and so a conference would be inappropriate in the school setting.

Rarely, though, in the chaos of the school day, do any of us have the time to answer one vital question with regard to our own school response: "What outcome are we seeking to achieve?"

Do we want this matter dealt with quickly? Quietly? Do we need to show the school community that we mean business? Is there pressure from some sections of the staff or school council to get "serious" with wrongdoers? Do we want to make an example of this case to act as a deterrent to others? Are we being rational or emotional in our decision-making? Is it simply a matter of determining what rule has been broken, and therefore what punishment applies?

Or are we, as a school community, concerned with using every opportunity to educate young people about the consequence of their actions for others as well as for themselves?

If the school has adopted a restorative, relational approach to the management of behaviour, then the questions that will be asked in the wake of such an incident might be:

"Who is responsible and accountable for what has happened?"

"Which community of people has been affected?"

"What might their needs be?"

"What is the extent of the harm that has been done?"

"How might we begin to repair that harm?"

"How can we get the young wrongdoer to face up to what he/she has done?"

"Who are the best people to do that?"

"How might we prevent this happening again?"

"What's important here? That we show the school community that the young wrongdoer has been punished? Or that we seek to facilitate the repair of the damage to individuals and relationships?"

These questions can be asked even more simply:

"Has harm been done? Is there a need to repair the harm? Do we have the time to make this investment in our school community? Can we afford not to?"

A community conference should not be considered if the person accused of misconduct denies that they have been involved in the incident. The process does not and should not resemble a court of law, an arena where the facts of a case in dispute can be decided by a jury. Neither is it appropriate for a conference to be used as an investigative tool to discover previously unknown facts, so that young people can be punished further. So if there is a clear "yes" to the question "Has the young person admitted to the wrongdoing?", then there is a clear mandate on the part of decision-makers to proceed with further considerations. These might include:

- How many people have been involved?

- What is the potential benefit of a conference to this community?

- What is the potential benefit to the young wrongdoer and his/her family?

- What is the nature and seriousness of the wrongdoing?

- Has the young person a history of previous misconduct?

- What have we tried so far? Has it worked?

- What are the risks of going ahead with a conference?

- What are the risks of not going ahead with a conference?

All of the questions detailed in this section impose a degree of responsibility on the shoulders of the decision-maker. In our experience, this decision is best shared by a group of people who can "nut out" the issues outlined above. This works best when those people are familiar with the philosophy and practice of restorative measures such as conferencing.

Pilots of conferencing in schools have also highlighted inconsistencies in decision-making based largely on differences in beliefs, attitudes, stereotyping and our own emotional responses to individual students, their parents and the nature of the incident.

The reasons schools have used a punitive approach in preference to a restorative approach include:

- Not enough time

- The community here expects it (punishment) of us

- The wrongdoer will not respond positively to a conference

- The family of the wrongdoer is dysfunctional

- It didn't occur to us at the time

- These decisions are the responsibility of one person

- What's happened is so disgusting, it needs to be punished

- It's too complicated

- We must follow the state/county discipline policy – this covers our accountability

What is not stated openly because it is not understood, is that when we are faced with a student who shows contempt for authority (angry rejection) we can fall very quickly into the trap of wanting to retaliate. And the most familiar way to do that in the school community is to punish our wrongdoer by stigmatising, isolating and/or incapacitating him/her. The risk, of course, is that we further alienate those very students and their families who are our most vulnerable, and who may later cause more harm in our communities.

> *"Has harm been done? Is there a need to repair the harm? Do we have the time to make this investment in our school community? Can we afford not to?"*

Be aware that a common trap in deciding not to go ahead with a conference is often a subconscious thought that the young person does not "deserve" a conference, based on his or her attitude, or a history of previous misconduct. These young people are those who are most in need of the opportunity to redeem themselves and to make some serious decisions about the direction their life is taking.

If your decision is based solely on how you feel about the wrongdoer, you have ignored the needs of the whole community of people affected by the incident or behaviour. The solution here is to focus on the incident rather than on the wrongdoer/s. You may need to remind decision-makers of the key questions:

"Has harm been done? Is there a need to repair the harm? Do we have the time to make this investment in our school community? Can we afford not to? What else works?"

> *... conferencing is not a soft option for wrongdoers.*

And finally, it is our experience that conferencing is not a soft option for wrongdoers. Students have commented that they would prefer to be suspended from school rather than face up to a group of affected people, as the conference is "real tough". ■

Chapter 3

Conference preparation

If your school has been using restorative processes for some time, staff, students and parents will come to expect a conference as the "normal" way of resolving more serious difficulties. If your school is "new" to this approach, then the process of convincing people may take a little more time.

If the decision has been made by the school administration/executive to proceed with a conference, key parties need to be consulted about whether they would be willing to participate. It is a good idea to check first with the victim and his/her family. You will need to carefully explain the process and its benefits and any alternatives. They will need to be convinced that a conference is an appropriate course of action, that they will not be further victimised and that their issues will be addressed. The next key party to consult with will be the wrongdoer and his/her parents. If they, too, can be convinced that the process has benefits for them and that their issues can be resolved, then you can proceed with the organisation of the conference. Do not exclude teaching staff from these explanations. They will be attending a conference in a particular role of victim, supporter, witness or, sometimes, wrongdoer. Their needs are no different!

Step 1: Establishing the facts and deciding who comes

The obvious place to start is with the school official who has been conducting the investigation. Ask:

■ What happened?

■ Who was involved?

■ What has happened since?

These facts will give you, the facilitator, a general idea about who needs to be invited to the conference, and how the conference is to be used.

■ Is it to become the "ceremony of reintegration" for the young wrongdoers who have been suspended?

■ Is it a case of "show cause why your enrolment should not be terminated"?

■ Is it a process to be used to tackle an ongoing issue?

■ Is it to be used as an appeal process against a decision made by the school board to exclude a student?

This, of course, raises the issue of timing. Common practice dictates that a conference will usually be

> *Remember it is the community of people affected by the incident who need to be involved in the repair of the harm and the resolution of issues. Put simply, this community consists of "those who did it, and those who had it done to them".*

held around five days after an incident, or at the conclusion of a suspension, to give the school and facilitator time to organise it. Too soon after an incident will mean that potential participants will not have had time to make meaning of the event or gather their emotional resources; too long afterwards may mean that the moment is lost. Having said that, however, you may have to convene a conference virtually "on the spot" or indeed weeks and months after an event which is still preying on the mind of a victim or their parents. Use your judgement and keep in mind the usual questions: Has the wrongdoer admitted to the wrongdoing? Has harm been done? Is there still a need to repair the damage so that people are afforded some closure and healing is possible?

You will then need to interview these key people (students, staff, parents/caregivers) so that you can make a judgement about whether others may need to be invited. These people may have had some part to play, or can shed some light on the circumstances. Remember it is the community of people affected by the incident who need to be involved in the repair of the harm and the resolution of issues. Put simply, this community consists of "those who did it, and those who had it done to them".

The list of participants usually includes:

- The victim(s)

- The victim's supporters, usually family/ caregivers (mother, father, siblings, grandparents, aunts, uncles) and friends or colleagues

- The wrongdoer(s)

- The wrongdoer's supporters – again, usually family, friends or colleagues

- Witnesses to the incident who may have been deeply affected

- School officials (Principal, Deputy) who have become involved in their role as investigators, or made the decision to suspend or exclude

- Staff (school counsellor, school chaplain) who may play a role in the future support of any of the parties

- Agency staff who may already be supporting the victim or the wrongdoer

- School board members if the conference is a "show cause" or appeal process

A word about supporters: this is a group of people who play a vital role in the conference. This is the group who can best disapprove of the behaviour that has caused the harm, but in a spirit of care and support. Not only does the problem behaviour cause rifts in the relationships in the wrongdoer's community of care, it can also deeply disrupt the relationships in the victim's family and relationships in staff rooms where staff have been closely involved. One hoped-for outcome of the conference is to reintegrate young people (or indeed the adults present) back into their respective communities of care, and into the school community. Relationships need to be repaired. Those parties most in need of repair need to be present at the conference.

It is also the case that some young people do not have the kind of community of care in their lives that can support them effectively through a difficult time. They may not live with family. You may think that the alcoholic mother or the unemployed father will not have anything to offer the conference process. Do not make the mistake of thinking that because the circumstances of the student are already compromised, their families, however "dysfunctional", have nothing to offer. However, it might be necessary for you to construct a community of care around a particular young person. In this case ask the young person who is significant to them and by whom they would feel supported. Call on teaching or welfare staff or any other adult or young person with whom you can see the potential for a lasting connection.

It is also important to select those people amongst staff and the wrongdoer's family and wider circle with whom the young wrongdoer has the deepest emotional connections. This person might be a sports coach, a favourite teacher, a close family friend, a favourite uncle, a grandmother. It is his/her need to repair these particular relationships that will make the difference to whether the wrongdoer responds positively during the conference.

Step 2: Interviewing participants before the conference

The purpose of these interviews is twofold. Firstly to gather information and explain the process, and secondly to build a trusting relationship between you, the facilitator and the participants.

This is best done face-to-face, but in some cases it may not be possible because of work commitments of those outside the school community. A phone call may be the only opportunity. It might need to be after hours. It is VITAL that you have interviewed all participants prior to the conference. You must explain the process and its purpose, the benefits and alternatives, so that people have a reasonable idea about what to expect. It may be helpful to provide participants with an information sheet about the conference process during your discussions (see 'Information for community conference participants' in the Appendix). If the circumstances are complicated (they often are), you must have a clear idea of all the issues and what it is that you are likely to hear during the conference.

In some cases, you may need to convince parents to put their decision to refer the matter to police or their lawyer on hold, until they can experience the conference and its outcomes. Concentrate on discovering what needs they believe will be met by involving other professionals. Explain how the conference might better meet those needs. It will be important to manage the expectations of potential participants. Some will want to use the process to "savage" a young wrongdoer, a teacher, deputy principal or the institution itself. Others will believe that the process will produce fundamental changes in the behaviour of a persistent wrongdoer. Explain carefully that one to two hours involvement in a process such as a conference will not reverse the damage of a compromised upbringing. This particular model of conferencing is incident centred,

> *A golden rule for facilitators:
> NO SURPRISES! Do your best to know
> all the stories ahead of the conference.
> Leave nothing to chance.*

not wrongdoer centred.

You also need to know what particular stories need to be aired on the day to bring the whole group to an understanding of the harm done and the underlying

circumstances, so that the process unfolds as it should. A golden rule for facilitators: NO SURPRISES! Do your best to know all the stories ahead of the conference. Leave nothing to chance. And in spite of all that preparation, you will continually be surprised by some of the things you will hear, or what dynamics might unfold.

Sometimes, you will have unexpected guests at a conference: someone who initially refused to participate, a neighbour or family friend who has come to support a mother. Delay the start of the conference until you have briefed them about the process and its purpose and try to find out what their issues are. Again, operate on the principle of "no surprises".

The questions that are useful to ask during these interviews are pretty much the same as in the script:

- *What's your involvement?*
- *What did you think when you first heard?*
- *What's happened since?*
- *How are things at home? In the classroom? In the staffroom?*
- *How has this affected you?*
- *What are the issues that concern you the most?*
- *Have you thought about what you need now?*

Many participants will need reassuring that they will be emotionally and physically safe during and after a conference. This is especially true in instances of violence and bullying, when victims and their families worry about retribution for "dobbing". While this may indeed be a risk where schools choose to punish perpetrators, in our experience the risk of backlash in the wake of a conference, where the focus is on repair rather than punishment, is very much reduced. Assure them that if they have concerns about this, they can bring them up during the conference, and the issues can be resolved, and the agreement used, to record a plan to minimise the chance of revictimisation.

You may also judge that some of the conference participants could benefit from coaching before the conference. Young people will benefit by rehearsing their answers to the specific questions that you will be asking them in the conference. Tell them what you think it will be useful for the group to hear. This is usually very reassuring for victims and hesitant participants. Teachers, for example, may be reluctant to share their true feelings about what has happened and how it has affected them. This is based on a belief shared by some that if they tell a student how inadequate they feel, how they believe they are failing to do their job properly, how they blame themselves for not being able to cope or manage, or show their vulnerability, they will be taken advantage of. Some parents may be afraid of crying, or exploding in anger. Reassure people that you are there to manage the tough bits, and that it is the sharing of feelings and thoughts that brings empathy and insight to the whole group that is gathered at the conference.

The school executive may also need to be coached about the use of "schoolspeak". Principals and deputies need to be convinced of the need to shy away from utterances about the "school reputation" and other abstract comments about the institution, and be prepared to talk about their sleepless nights, the distractions, their hurt, disappointment and worry. This is more likely to penetrate the defences of a young person than any reference to the abstract, or the system which they may believe has failed them anyway.

Step 3: Arranging a time and venue and refreshments

This may well be the most frustrating part of your conference preparation, or indeed the conference itself! Getting a diverse group of people together at a mutually agreeable time can be a challenge. Some may not have transport, and you may have to offer to pick them up and take them home or to work afterwards. Some parents work hours that do not match the school day. Some people will baulk at attending because they need more information about what will happen in the conference. If you do your preparation well, most will be keen to participate and will usually make sacrifices to attend. Consider doing the conference before school, late in the afternoon, or in the evening, so that the majority of key participants can attend.

Some participants may have very young children, and may not be able to arrange babysitting. Have a collection of toys in the room, or arrange for a senior student to mind small children in a room close by. Be prepared to have very small children in the room during the conference. It might be anticipated that this could be a major distraction, but in fact it is rarely the case. Experience has shown us that these minor obstacles can be overcome with tolerance and common sense.

People need to know how long the conference will take. Classes may need to be covered, students

excused from their own classes, arrangements made with employers for time off work. A standard conference with 12 – 15 participants should take around two hours (this includes refreshments at the close). Positive outcomes for all participants are more likely when all of them can stay for the entire process. Remind participants to turn off their mobile phones.

The choice of venue needs some careful thought. The school may have a private room, where interruptions can be prevented, and which is big enough to seat participants in same-size chairs in a circle. Some parents, though, for reasons related to their own early experiences at school may be more comfortable in neutral territory. A district or regional office conference room might be a possibility. A community hall or reception centre may need to be hired. In some cases, the parents of the victim or wrongdoer may be so angry that the very fact that the school is prepared to take the conference "off site" will convince them that the school is taking the matter very seriously.

Ensure that the venue has photocopying resources available. The agreement is signed by all present, and copies are provided to all of these people, usually before they leave. Facilitators may choose to have the blank agreement form formatted on school letterhead, others may choose blank paper. Your school will, no doubt, develop its own preferred practice over time.

> *The opportunity for ongoing reintegration and reconnection between participants should not be terminated in a hurry.*

Provide refreshments at the conclusion of the conference. The opportunity for ongoing reintegration and reconnection between participants should not be terminated in a hurry. You will need time to write up the agreement in any case, and this can be done while people are chatting over a cup of tea, a sandwich or an orange juice. "Breaking bread with the enemy" after a tough couple of hours together has a powerful, although often subconscious, healing effect. The impact of a successful conference will be felt long after the formal part of the conference is over, and may take weeks and months.

Conference seating plan

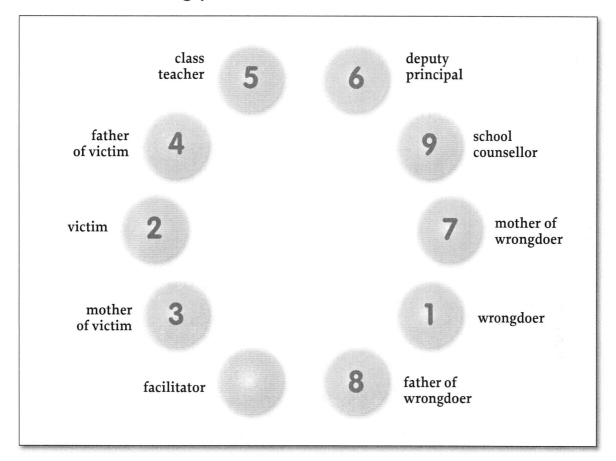

An example of a conference seating plan with sequence of questioning indicated by numbers

Step 4: Drawing a seating plan

Unless you are in the unusual position of having only a few people at a conference, developing a seating plan will be every bit as useful to you in managing the process as the conference script. Common practice again dictates that wrongdoers and their supporters sit on one side of the circle, facing the victim and their supporters. More neutral parties, such as the investigating officer and the school counsellor who might be there to provide further support, will usually be seated between the two groups. As can be seen from the seating plan diagram, it is important to surround the victim and the wrongdoer with their support group. As reconnection and reintegration are primary goals of the process, we cannot allow individuals to feel any more alienated or isolated than they already are.

Beginning conference facilitators often worry about losing their way in the process. It has proved helpful (even for experienced facilitators) to write numbers against the names in your seating plan to indicate the order in which you plan to engage participants. If the group is large, use colour coding to help you recognise who belongs to which group. Keeping the order right as per the script is important if you wish to keep the process on track.

If numbers are too large, for practical reasons you may decide to have an inner circle and an outer circle. Those in the inner circle are the main community affected by the incident, those in the outer circle are 'extra' supporters. Because of time only a few of these supporters will be asked to speak. If this is your plan, be very explicit with the support group about who is going to speak and who must be silent. Remind students to be silent with their body language if they are in the outer circle. With issues of bullying and harassment, be alert to 'death stares' from supporters. An imbalance of supporters will not be an issue if you stick to the script and conference plan. Conference circles with up to 35 participants are not a problem. Room size and eye contact need to

Restorative Practices in Schools

be considered with these large groups.

You may also consider, if the numbers are large, or the matter is particularly complex, to co-facilitate. This might happen in either of two ways: you split the script between you, so that one of you might do the introductions and questioning of the wrongdoer; the other might deal with the harm done and formulating the agreement. The other option is to nominate one facilitator to manage the flow of the script, while the other pursues key comments made by participants in order to get a better understanding of issues and circumstances.

For example, you might indicate that you want to interrupt by saying:

"Could I just ask a question here? Jane, you just said that your Dad had told you to 'sort it out today' as you left for school that morning. What do you think he meant by that?"

Step 5: Preparing for likely dynamics

It is sometimes the case that the people involved in a conference have had a long association with each other which may have been positive or negative. When parents of either the victim or the wrongdoer come from the same small community outside the school, it is quite possible that they already know each other. There may be a long history of conflict, which has surfaced between children at the school. Parents may have strong opinions about a particular teacher who may previously have taught one of their other children. A family may have a history of violence in a neighbourhood, and some may be in fear for their personal safety in the wake of a conference. Be aware of these dynamics. Do your best to understand this previous history because it will have an impact on the conference. If you haven't planned for it, it could derail the process. If you have a school-based police officer, invite him/her to attend. Again, predicting what might happen will help you develop a contingency plan and you will be able to maintain your poise. Hopefully, the conference can be the opportunity for families, or at least their children, to make peace.

It is also likely that during the course of the interviews the school and its staff will come in for some criticism – about processes, policies, practices or attitudes and behaviours of those staff or administrators involved in the incident(s). There may well be criticism that the school has neglected some aspect of its duty of care. We think the raising of these issues to be entirely fair, as a conference is about collective responsibility for offending behaviour. The conference highlights aspects of the school system or culture which have contributed to the problem. If we are insisting that students are accountable for their actions, then so must we accept our share of the responsibility. The restorative justice philosophy emphasises collective accountability and collective responsibility. The best way to put this information to constructive use is to have these concerns aired during the conference and addressed in the agreement.

If you are aware that such criticism may be revealed in the conference it would be valuable to discuss these with those school administrators who are participants ahead of the conference. Some may be reluctant to go ahead with the conference; others will appreciate the overture and that you have avoided a perceived ambush. You may need to remind them of the philosophy and approach (heart talk rather than administrator talk) so that they can participate effectively.

Using an interpreter

Conflict is sometimes an issue in schools which are multi-racial, particularly where countries of origin may be sworn enemies. There may be occasions where some participants, particularly parents, do not use English as their first language. If you wish to engage the parents and possibly key members of an ethnic community, you will have to consider using an interpreter. It will be important for you to establish the capacity of the interpreter to remain neutral, and to be acceptable to all ethnic groups represented at the conference. Spend time with the interpreter to explain the process, its hoped-for outcomes, and any issues they might believe could impede progress towards those goals. Impress on them that they can have no agenda in the process other than helping people better understand each other.

These conferences will take much longer, so prepare people for this. Use home–school liaison officers, social workers or school youth workers to assist you in convincing reluctant starters to attend. Be aware of cultural differences, especially about issues that risk shaming families further, or of how hard it might be for them to express their feelings when they may not be used to such public disclosures. They will need to be reassured of their safety, and that of their children. ■

Chapter 4

Convening the conference

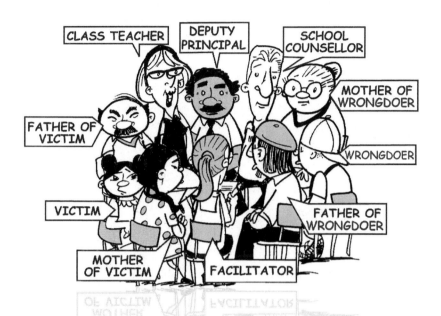

Greeting the participants on arrival

To avoid discomfort and increased anxiety for any of the conference participants, whether they belong to the victim or wrongdoer group, move parties to separate rooms until everyone has arrived. Place one group in the room where the conference will occur. The other group might assemble, for example, in a classroom or a deputy principal's office nearby. You may want to have a colleague assisting with greeting people and ushering them into separate rooms. This will allow you to focus on the facilitator's role and to speak to those participants who may still need some reassurance. If people arrive unexpectedly, take them aside to discover their reasons for attending, and to explain the purpose of the conference. Show people where the amenities are. This may prevent later interruptions or discomfort. As soon as all parties have arrived, seat people quickly and begin the conference.

Using the conference script

The script represents a plan to assist you in managing the process of the conference. As a beginner, you would be well served to stick closely to the questions and their particular sequence. As you grow more experienced, you may find it easier to adapt the script slightly to a particular set of circumstances, but the fundamental purpose, the type of questions and the sequence of those questions ought to remain unchanged. Experience has shown us that getting the order of participant involvement right is one of the critical factors in determining positive outcomes. Playing with the sequence will make your job much harder as you risk the process going awry. As you facilitate the conference, always have the conference script with you as part of the paperwork on your lap along with the seating plan and a blank agreement. Refer to the script when you get stuck or need an opportunity to allow participants to quietly reflect on a significant moment.

The introduction sets the scene and places you, the facilitator, in the driving seat. It also, importantly, reminds people of the purpose of the conference: that is, to acknowledge what harm has been done, to seek ways to repair that harm and minimise the chance of it happening again. It also reminds people that the purpose of the conference is not to judge anyone, but rather to talk about the impact of the behaviours on others. This is also worthwhile remembering when the dynamics of the conference become "interesting" and the group moves away from this central task and philosophy. A timely reminder of the purpose is usually enough to refocus participants.

Conference script 1: introduction

As it is written, the script has you, the facilitator, performing the introductions. In some cultures, it may be more appropriate to allow people to introduce themselves. Be wary, however, of cultural practice which may lead to long-winded introductions and/or participants who use the opportunity to take "pot-shots" at others in the group. There is nothing to be gained at the early stages of the conference in allowing the group to take over the process. Most issues around cultural differences can be ironed out in pre-conference negotiations. For some groups, starting the process with a prayer or song is important. Rule of thumb – go with what allows people to feel appropriately respected, while you stay in charge.

Script

Welcome. As you know, my name is _____, and I will be coordinating this conference. Before the conference begins, I would like to introduce everybody briefly and indicate their reasons for being here.

Another version might look like this:

I want to thank everybody for being here today. Some of you are missing out on your lunchtime/meeting time/sport practice/time with your family/planning other school activities. Before we start I want to go around the group and explain why people are here today.

At this stage, I would like to thank you all for making the effort to attend. This is a difficult (and/or complicated/sensitive) matter, and your participation here will help us deal with it.

The conference will focus on the incident (eg the assault) which happened (last Tuesday at the bus stop), involving (wrongdoer's and victim's names).

It's important to understand that we will focus on what (wrongdoer's name) did and how his/her behaviour has affected others. We are not here to decide whether (wrongdoer's name) is a good or bad person. We want to explore how people have been affected, and see whether we can begin to repair the harm that has been done.

Explanation

The introductions are usually performed in order around the circle.

This allows you to describe the role of each person in this community of people affected by the incident, eg "On my right is Mr Giani, father of Michael, one of the boys involved in the assault. On his right is Michael, and next to him is Mrs Mackie, who is Dean of the year 8 student body, and is here today to support Michael and his family..."

We believe that with young people, the introduction of 'why they are at the conference' is important. Even though all of the students and teachers present may know each other, the introduction is an explicit statement of 'who did what to whom' and does not allow the wrongdoers, victims or supporters to deviate from their involvement, or to mitigate any responsibility. It also reduces pressure on the facilitator to draw out each story or admission from each participant.

If the conference is being convened to deal with a series of incidents over time, in which the "wrongdoer" on one day is the "victim" the next – eg chronic conflict – it might be beneficial to include all the young people's names in this introduction.

Script

Alternatively:

We are all here today to talk about what happened... when ... who ... We are not going to talk about ... and ... as good or bad people, we are only going to talk about what they did. Today we need to find out what happened and why, and what harm has been caused by this incident. All of us here today will help to repair the harm and to make an agreement that will make sure that this does not happen again. When this agreement is reached, it will be the end of this conference. If ... , ... and ... stick to the agreement, the school will do nothing more. You will all be given a chance to tell your story. Everyone in turn will have a chance to be heard. This means that we will be here for about 2 hours. Is that OK?

(To wrongdoer/s): *..., you have admitted your involvement in the incident. If at any stage during the conference you no longer wish to participate, you are free to leave – but if you choose to do so, the matter will be dealt with differently. This matter will be finished when this conference is over and you have completed what people ask you to do to repair the harm. Is that clear?*

Alternatively:

You can leave the conference any time you like, but if you do you need to know that what you did will be handled differently by the school. Do you understand this?

Explanation

For instance:

"We will be focusing on a series of events since the beginning of term in which Michael, Jeremy, Bill and Jordan have been involved to some degree or other – the latest of which culminated in the assault which took place last Tuesday at the bus stop. We are not here to decide if any of these young people are good or bad. We are more interested in understanding what has happened, how it came to get so out of hand, what harm has been done, how we might repair that harm, and more importantly, how we might reach agreement to make sure this sort of thing doesn't happen again."

The meaning of "differently" will vary with each circumstance. Whatever the reason, it must be clarified with participants before the conference, and at this point of the process on the day. It may be that the parents of a victim of assault, for example, have put their decision to refer the matter to the police on hold, pending the outcome of the conference. The conference may be convened as a "show cause" meeting for a final decision about whether or not a student should remain in the school. The conference may be convened as an avenue of appeal against a Board of Trustee decision to exclude a student.

Conference script 2: questioning the wrongdoer(s)

Telling the story

This first phase of the conference is vital and must not be rushed (a temptation for beginning facilitators). It begins to paint the picture of what happened and the circumstances which led to the incident or incidents. It is crucial that the questioning technique used does not deteriorate into something resembling the Spanish Inquisition! Rather, be quietly persistent in your questioning and pursuit of the whole story.

Where there is confusion about the facts, seek clarification. Remember, the young people who have done the wrong thing have already admitted their part in it. This no longer has to be proved. We are trying to understand their motivation and decision-making capacity. Victims need to understand why it has happened to them. We are also seeking to understand the life circumstances of the wrongdoer; these young people are often the most vulnerable despite outward appearances and attitude. These stories can provide clues about what kind of support can be built into the final agreement.

Because your preparation has been so careful, and you know everyone's stories, you will have a sense of which extra questions you may need to ask of any participant at any stage in the conference. Often, important events have occurred amongst that group that need to be brought out at the conference. It is very acceptable to prompt participants so that these 'social markers' are heard.

For example:

"Peter, when we talked about your involvement in this before the conference, you said that you told your mates that you didn't want to be involved any longer in what was happening. Can you tell us about that?"

It may sometimes appear that wrongdoers are reluctant to tell their stories. It is useful to remember how very confronting it might be for a young person facing a large group of people, and they may well be very nervous. And young people are not as articulate as adults. You may have to work hard to elicit the story.

Script

Wrongdoer(s):

... to help us understand what harm has been done and who has been affected by this incident, could you start by telling us what happened?

Explanation

The direction "tell us what happened" may not be a one-off. You may need to ask the question many times until you are satisfied that the whole story has unfolded.

eg "... and then what happened?"

or, "Can we go back to the beginning again, there's a bit I don't quite understand. Talk about what was happening in the maths class before you were asked to leave"

or "How were you feeling when you woke that morning and realised that you would have to get on that same bus with him again?"

Where there are multiple wrongdoers, you can decide whether to use all the questions on each wrongdoer before moving on, or use one

question and move through all wrongdoers one at a time.

Often it is useful to begin a question with a statement that allows for no ambiguity:

"When you punched Sally in the face, what were you thinking/feeling? What had been happening that morning?"

Script

■ *How did you come to be involved?*

■ *What were you thinking at the time?*

Or

■ *What made you decide to do that?*

■ *How did you come to decide to do that?*

■ *What was going on in your head at the time?*

■ *What have you thought about since the incident?*

Or

■ *What have you thought about since this has all happened?*

Explanation

The answers may well build our understanding of antecedent circumstances and also help us to understand the pressures in the young person's life. It may be that a previous relationship existed where two parties were firm friends, and then something happened to sour the relationship. It sometimes happens that two families in the community have a history of conflict which is now impacting at school. Make sure though, when you ask this question, that you already know the answer (from pre-conference interviews).

This question is critical to reaching an understanding of the motivation behind a particular act. It is tempting to ask "why did you do it?" in these circumstances because victims often have a strong need to know that answer. However, a more useful question is the one that searches for antecedent circumstances and/or the young person's decision-making processes. These may well have been flawed in our eyes, but make perfect sense in his/her world. The group will have their answer to "why" when the young person answers the question.

It might be useful to ask, as well, "and how were you feeling at the time?" if they have not already shared that with you in answering the first question. People often give "feeling" answers to "thinking" questions, although boys may need some help with this.

You are likely to get a variety of answers here, depending on the capacity of the young person for self-reflection, and their maturity. Some may already be remorseful about their actions. Others may be angry that they have got into trouble, or at how unfairly they feel they have been treated. Others may not understand why there has been such a fuss. There are no right or wrong answers here – just a window for us to see into their thinking. With young people who have not been able to reflect on their actions, it is useful to move on and revisit this question after hearing from the victims.

Script

- *Who do you think has been affected by your actions and in what way?*

Explanation

This will give the conference participants another insight into the emotional/social maturity of the wrongdoer. Some young people will have very little understanding about the depth and breadth of the harm that has been done. They may well respond with answers such as "Mum was really upset" or "He was probably angry with me". You will have to use your judgement at this point about whether or not to pursue the wrongdoer's understanding of the harm, or let the conference process do the job as planned. This is where the conference is a powerful tool for conscience building and teaching about cause and effect.

Conference script 3: exploring the harm

The purpose of this part of the conference is to build understanding about the depth and breadth of the harm done. The whole conference 'community' now has a chance to share their feelings and thoughts about what has happened before, during and after the incident. It is as if each participant has a piece of a giant jigsaw puzzle, and in laying his/her story out for the whole group to hear, a shared understanding about harm can be reached. This part of the conference is the core 'lesson' for wrongdoers who have not yet shown remorse or understanding about the harm caused to people and relationships. This is the beginning, for them, of lessons in empathy, self-reflection, developing a sense of right and wrong and taking responsibility for their behaviour and its impact on others.

The order in which people are invited to tell their stories is critical: victims first, then their supporters, followed by the parents/caregivers of the wrongdoer, then their supporters. It is imperative that parents of the wrongdoer(s) hear others' stories before talking about their own experiences. If the wrongdoer's parents are invited to speak before hearing these stories, there is a strong chance that they will defend their son or daughter before they are in possession of all the facts. This risks derailing the process, because it will likely antagonise the victim's party and raise the emotional temperature of the conference unnecessarily.

In incidents which have no apparent victim (eg drug related incidents, or truancy), start with the people who became involved over time – that is, follow the chronology of events. In the case of students being caught with drugs or alcohol at school or away at camp, start with the adult who discovered what was happening, then proceed to the next person who had to be informed, and so on. With truancy, involve those who have to become involved – teachers, administrative support staff, school based police. They will have strong feelings about the behaviour. Do not make up pseudo victims. Victims need to be real people, not administrative reputations or school images.

Script

Victims:

- *What did you think at the time?*

- *What have you thought about since?*

- *How has this incident affected you?*

- *How did your family and friends react when they heard about the incident?*

Sometimes when people are very distressed, or very angry, a helpful question is:

- *What has been the worst of it for you?*

Or

- *What are the main issues here for you?*

Explanation

An alternative question here might be "how has this changed how you feel about coming to school?" or "how has this changed things with your friends?" Because you know from your interviews something in particular, you might ask leading questions such as "how has this affected things at home?" or "what has been the personal cost to you?" If the victim is a young person, they may well not have the linguistic skills to describe their state adequately. Do not worry too much about this because their parents or caregivers will be able and willing to do this. Be prepared to change the language of the questions you ask to suit the maturity/age of the young person.

If the person being questioned here is a teacher, the question might be adapted to "How did the other teachers in your staffroom react?" If the person being questioned is a Board member, or a member of the Parent Association, alter the question appropriately.

Where the victims include adults (teacher, school principal, canteen convenor, camp co-ordinator), it is vital that they be encouraged to share with others the emotional component of the harm, ie how they FEEL and the pressures/stress they may be suffering as a result. They may need to be coached before the conference to be willing to share this personal information. It is just this personal sharing and vulnerability/humanity which is more likely to have an impact on wrongdoers and their parents than any rational "schoolspeak".

Script

Victim supporters:

- *What did you think when you heard about the incident?*

- *How do you feel about what has happened?*

- *What has happened since?*

Or

- *What changes have you seen in your son/daughter?*

Or

- *What changes have you seen in your colleague?*

- *As ...'s parent/friend/colleague, what has been the hardest for you?*

- *What are the main issues here for you?*

Wrongdoer supporters:

- *It must be difficult for you to hear this.*

- *What did you think when you heard?*

- *How do you feel about what has happened?*

- *What has happened since?*

- *How has it affected you?*

- *How are things at home? How are things now between you all?*

- *What has been the worst of all this for you?*

Explanation

This is the group which will be comprised mainly of parents/caregivers and friends/colleagues of the primary victim. This group is likely to be deeply upset about what has happened, possibly very angry. To afford any relief to this group, it is vital that they be encouraged to talk about how they feel about what has happened. Parents are particularly vulnerable to feeling helpless in the face of an injury to their son or daughter, and this may often be masked by strong displays of anger. The questions should allow the supporter group to express these strong feelings.

This section of the conference is very important because this is the point at which the young wrongdoer is more likely to take notice of the harm they have done to those to whom they are most closely connected.

This group will most likely be parents/close relatives or significant adults in the young person's life. It is also possible that they will be defensive about their son/daughter's actions, and/or deeply upset. The first statement is an acknowledgement of this.

If they express surprise, explore why this is so. It will provide those present with a window into the young wrongdoer's whole persona, rather than just the bit that has caused the harm.

If parents/caregivers are highly critical of their child, it may be useful to explore other parts of their behaviour/persona which indicate a positive relationship or to enlist the support of others in the room to find some positive feedback for the young wrongdoer.

Remember that no matter how awful the wrongdoer's actions have been, parents will, most times, be their advocate. The shame and humiliation they experience as primary carers may be directed at the school.

"This school/teacher always picks on her, no wonder she did this."

Script

Explanation

Be patient with this defensiveness. This response can be a mask for their own shame about how they may have failed as a parent. Allow the group to engage the parents in a discussion about the rightness or wrongness of the behaviour. If the defensive responses persist, ask:

"What do you really think/feel about what s/he did?"

"Do you think that behaviour is acceptable?"
Be aware that in some families, one parent may be in the habit of dominating discussion. If you can pick this up in the pre-conference interviews, direct questions first to the less dominant parent, so they get a chance to express their views and feelings before being overwhelmed by the other partner. If one partner continually interrupts or overrides the other say:

"I know this is hard for you, but it's important that we hear from Tony's mum right now."

Conference script 4: acknowledgement and apology

This is the moment in the conference where the wrongdoer is given the space in which to demonstrate that they have understood, at least in part, who has been harmed by their actions and in what way. For the victims, it is most important to hear this acknowledged. Wait for the response. Use silence.

Victims have four primary questions that need to be

answered through the course of the conference:

■ *Why me?*

■ *Do you understand how you have affected me?*

■ *Are you sorry for the things that you have done to me?*

■ *Will you do this to me again?*

If the facilitator has followed the script in questioning the wrongdoer, so that motivation and circumstance are understood, victims will have had some answers.

Script

Wrongdoer:

Now that you've heard from everybody about how they've been affected by what you've done, is there anything you want to say to ... (the victim), or anyone else here?

If necessary:

Is there something... (victim, parents, teacher, etc), needs to hear from you right now?

Explanation

Owning their behaviour, acknowledging the harm ("I didn't realise"), and showing genuine remorse ("I'm sorry") places them at the "mercy" of those present, and assists in the next stage of planning to make amends. Some young people, who have poor social skills or lack any degree of emotional awareness and are unable to "read the play", may have to be directed/ assisted by you or others at the conference, to make the appropriate response.

Conference script 5: agreement

This begins the stage of the conference where plans are made to repair the harm (making amends), put support structures into place for those in need, and re-think some of the structures, policies and practices that may have contributed to the circumstances. If there are issues which have not been fully aired, or needs that have not yet been met, it will become apparent in this phase. Most victims will be satisfied with acknowledgement and apology and less concerned with material reparation if you have facilitated the conference by following the script. However, if the wrongdoer has not owned their behaviour, acknowledged the harm done, or provided a clear understanding to participants of the antecedents, then victims and their supporters will make unreasonable demands. If you sense lingering resentment and anger you may have to re-visit the script.

In some cultures in the criminal justice sector, it is practice to allow the wrongdoers and their supporters to meet privately to make their own decisions about this plan and to bring it back to the whole group for discussion and debate. In this model, however, negotiations are conducted with all participants present. You may choose to take suggestions from all parties before negotiating the final plan, or you may negotiate each item in the plan as it is presented. Always start with the primary victim. If his/her parents are in conflict with these wishes, give preference to the primary victim's wishes.

Your role as facilitator during negotiations is to assist people to come to a mutual agreement. If you wish to make a suggestion, ask the group if they would like to hear it, and then offer it in a very tentative way:

"Can I make a suggestion here that might be useful? I wonder if .... could happen? I do know that in other cases like this, it has been important that we consider... What do you all think?"

Script

To the victim and the victim supporters:

- *What do you want to see happen as a result of the conference/meeting today (or to repair the harm)?*

To wrongdoer and wrongdoer supporters:

- *Does that seem fair?*
- *Is there something that you would like to see happen that might help?*

Explanation

Allow plenty of time for discussion. As stated above, if this stage becomes heated, it will most likely be the case that people's needs have not yet been met. It might even be that a party's capacity to read genuine remorse on the part of the wrongdoer is impaired for some reason. A useful question to ask at this point might be "what needs to happen to convince you that she is genuinely sorry and that it will not happen again?"

It might be useful, too, to record in the agreement what will happen if the behaviour recurs, so that the wrongdoer is clear about future consequences. This will be a particular concern for victims of bullying.

It is also useful to ask the wrongdoer and his/her supporters for their ideas about how to make amends:

Script

Explanation

Take care that whatever is decided does not further shame the wrongdoer. The risk is that any gains made during the conference will be eroded by making him/her or the parents angry rather than thoughtful. This will be especially true for conferences which involve different cultural groups. If demands are made that wrongdoers or their parents object to, attempt to discover the need which underlies the request. For example, a common request is for students to make a public apology to the student body. Some people can cope with this. Others cannot or will not. If this is the case, find out what outcome is sought by this demand, and then ask if there is an alternative, more acceptable way this could be achieved.

Make certain that items in the agreement are realistically achievable, and written in language which is concrete and easily understood, eg

"Tina will assist special need students in the Special Needs unit on Tuesdays and Thursdays in the last half of her lunch hour for the next three weeks. She will report to Mrs Deagon on arrival."

It is sometimes the case that the group may worry about issues of confidentiality. You would know this before the conference and may choose to agree in the opening stages of the conference that what will be said and the outcomes will remain confidential. In situations where large groups of students are likely to want to know what happened for gossip's sake, you might suggest that, from past experience it is useful for all participants to agree to a common statement, for example:

"We've sorted everything out, and it's all over. We've all agreed not to say any more about it."

To all conference participants:

■ *Who will be responsible for supervising the terms of the agreement?*

The responsibility for monitoring the terms of the agreement will usually rest with a school administrator, counsellor or welfare staff at the conference. It is not usual that the conference facilitator has this responsibility.

This designated person can also provide ongoing practical and emotional support for the wrongdoer while he/she works towards meeting the terms of the agreement.

■ *Let me just summarise what you have agreed upon.*

You read the list of actions and get final agreement to commit it to paper.

Restorative Practices in Schools

Conference script 6: closing the conference

Script

You say to the whole group:

I will now record the agreement that's been reached here. This will formally close the matter, subject to completion of the agreement. You will each be asked to sign it and you will be given a copy before you leave.

Is there anything else anyone wants to say?

You have all worked hard to resolve this incident and the agreement you have reached should go a long way towards repairing the harm that has been done.

While I write down the agreement, which I will ask you all to sign before you leave, please enjoy the refreshments we have provided for you.

Explanation

Leave a little time for people to compose their thoughts, then speak.

It is important that this part of the conference is not rushed, and that people have an excuse to mingle a little longer before they leave. This is the informal reintegration phase that should extend well beyond the conference proper. Place yourself so that you can observe the dynamics. If any one particular person appears isolated

(they may feel too embarrassed to mingle) give some subtle cues to school staff to join them.

You may decide to ask a staff member to record the agreement while you mingle with conference participants. In any case, maintain a watch on the ongoing dynamics and give people every opportunity to reconnect. ■

Managing the
emotional dynamics

Formal discipline policy and procedures are designed to deliver "justice" to wrongdoers, that is, to sanction rule breaking behaviour by way of consequences which usually involve punishment. Most of these policies, which are driven by national, state, or county policy, are written after wide consultation with key stakeholders and much hard work on the part of a few. The focus is usually on the wrongdoer. But rarely in these deliberations do we ask how to deal with, or plan for, the emotional fallout of what happened, or how to deal with the needs of the rest of the community that has been harmed. At best those harmed are offered some counselling whilst wrongdoers may be directed toward anger management courses or social skills groups.

Because the restorative approach concentrates on understanding who has been hurt, what harm has been done and therefore what needs to happen to make amends and repair the damage, it is concerned with how people feel. So the conference (and any other restorative practice in the school) is the forum where feelings are attached to behaviours, and to the impact of those behaviours on the feelings of others. When you explore the nature of the questions in the script, you can see that people are invited to share their stories and experiences in a way which allows

the expression of emotion, often strong. Validation and acknowledgement of these feelings are important for allowing people to understand what has happened and why, come to terms with it, and achieve some sense of closure. Being understood is very powerful. When understanding happens, and wrongdoers accept responsibility for their behaviour and are genuinely remorseful, healing becomes possible.

Hence the transformative nature of the restorative approach.

When victims have a better understanding of the circumstances that led to the incident and why this happened to them, they are much less likely to demand punitive sanctions. This is especially true for teachers, who are often excluded from the decision about how to deal with an incident. Participants come to a conference feeling a range of emotions. Some will be seething with anger; some will be fearful; many will be distressed; some doubtful about the process and its hoped-for outcomes; some more cynical; some deeply ashamed of what's happened; others curious. The conference process will allow for the gradual transformation of these negative feelings into relief, hope, understanding, empathy, optimism and even enjoyment. There will be key moments during the conference where these transformations are obvious: when a young person finally understands how he/she has hurt family and friends or caused great distress and fear to another young person, when a student realises that his teacher is human after all, when a mother explains the obstacles she faces at home, and how desperately worried she is about her daughter and another participant reaches out in understanding.

When the conference begins, do not be put off by negative body language (arms and legs crossed, no eye contact, head down etc). This means that people have brought their emotions along. The conference is designed to transform these emotions. As the conference proceeds changes in body language will signal a change to interest as people become keen to contribute and participate. As your facilitation experience grows you will be able to observe body language and use it as a marker for conference progress and, possibly, unresolved issues. There are other moments in a conference when all the participants are hanging their heads and cannot bear to look at each other as they deal with their own shame and discomfort. People will make comments which inflame others. There are some people whose anger will not evaporate, and it appears that this might interfere with the healing.

> ***Extreme anger often masks a participant's deep shame.***

If you are aware that a particular person is especially angry, it might pay to seat them near you, so that you can, by the use of your own body language, help them to stay calm.

Since the conference is the forum in which people are afforded relief from very strong, often toxic emotions, it is important that we allow the expression of these. So, it is a fine line to walk between managing the dynamics of those who have a 'head of steam up' and need to unload, and managing the risk of derailing the dynamics by this prolonged anger interfering with the reconnection and healing that needs to happen. Because this open display of emotion may be very different and seem 'out of control' to some school administrators, it may be worthwhile to warn them before the conference. Reassure them that your facilitation and the process itself will manage these dynamics. This may assist them to participate rather than to regulate.

Extreme anger often masks a participant's deep shame: about not having been able to protect their son or daughter from harm; about the damage to their image of themselves as parents or teachers; about their perceptions of unfairness of policy or practice or treatment; about their perception that the wrongdoer is not truly sorry, that they have not yet understood, or appear not to care about what they have done.

It is important that you try to tap into these underlying causes when the anger persists to the point of interference. Some questions you might ask at this point might be:

> *Use silence.*

- ■ *"I can see that you are still very angry. Is there something that we are not understanding yet?"*
- ■ *"I know this is very difficult for you. What has been the worst of it?"*
- ■ *"You're saying that you think she is not sorry. What would need to happen to convince you that she is?"*

Affect psychology proposes a model to explain the range of human behaviour. People, including students, develop a life pattern to manage their shame, alienation, helplessness, isolation, rejection, humiliation – all the feelings which are quite normal in the wake of harmful behaviour or indeed contributed to the problem behaviour in the first instance. The behaviours which you may observe in a conference (or indeed any other dynamic in your personal or professional life) to manage these feelings of disconnection, fall into four categories:

- ■ **withdrawal** – people simply shut down as a way of coping
- ■ **avoidance** – people will attempt to divert the conversation away from that which is too painful by over-intellectualising or using "red herrings"
- ■ **attack self** – "this is all my fault", "I'm a bad parent"
- ■ **attack other** – anger and attacks on others in the group

Be aware of these possible patterns. You do not necessarily have to do anything with them when they arise, unless they begin to interfere with the course of the process. It helps to understand what you are witnessing so that you can maintain your poise in a difficult moment. Those of you who might wish to pursue a deeper understanding of these psycho/biological responses please refer to the recommended readings on affect psychology.

The other predominant emotion that often occurs in conferences is distress, usually in the form of tears. Do not try to stop someone crying. The expression of this particular emotion is as important as any other. Have a box of tissues with you. Give the person time to compose themselves. Use silence. Say "Take your time". Be prepared for the possibility that a person may need to leave the room to do this. Ask one of the school staff to go with them, provide comfort and reassurance, and to bring them back. If you can afford the time, suspend dialogue in the conference for the few minutes this will take. There may be other moments where someone will be quite overcome with other emotions such as anxiety, shame, disgust or possibly anger and will leave the room. The same rule applies. Send someone out to support them through the difficult moment and get them back into the conference as soon as possible.

> *Communities of people have an incredible capacity to manage their own affairs if they are provided with the opportunity and a direction.*

Understand, too, that people bring their own experiences and sometimes trauma and/or pathology with them to a conference. Not everyone who comes will be emotionally stable. We have found that increasing the number of participants in a conference will help minimise the risk of the difficulties that may arise as result of a participant's "baggage". This is one reason why it is so vital to interview participants beforehand, so that you can predict where the "hotspots" may occur, and therefore plan how to manage these. You may need to coach someone whom you regard as sensible and emotionally stable, to help manage the dynamic if it arises. It is often the case that the group itself will manage these challenges, with little input from you. A general "rule of thumb" is to include eight or more participants in a conference. Less increases the risk of limiting the range of emotional responses, and making your job harder.

Your goal, in fact, is to eventually become invisible. Your job, in a simple sense, is to facilitate difficult conversations between people, so that they can do

the repair work that is necessary in the wake of harmful behaviour. Communities of people have an incredible capacity to manage their own affairs if they are provided with the opportunity and a direction.

A caution for those facilitators who have counsellor training: conferences are not counselling sessions. They may be therapeutic, but they are not therapy. There will be little need for you to reflect, paraphrase or summarise (except with regard to the agreement) unless someone is really struggling to find a word. In fact, if you do, there is a risk that one party or another will become incensed with your attempts to demonstrate understanding of the other party's issues and feelings. When people share their thoughts and feelings with the whole group in answer to any question of yours, allow the group to make its own sense of what was said. Use silence. Give people time to process their own thoughts. The most effective skill you can use is to ask more questions (mostly open-ended), so that the responses can help build the shared understanding that is so necessary to the healing process.

For those of you with mediation training: a conference bears some resemblance to a mediation session, and mediation training may assist people to feel comfortable with the conference facilitator's role. Having said this, there are some major differences between the processes. Choosing which is appropriate for a situation is vital. Mediation assumes there is some common ground to form the basis of negotiating outcomes. In the case of harm being done, however, explaining to a victim that they will be participating in a process which assumes common ground with an wrongdoer is a shortcut to revictimisation. Another difference is that conferences involve participants outside the victim/wrongdoer community and include ideals of

collective responsibility and accountability.
Furthermore, conferences invite, engage and
manage strong emotion with the intention of
repairing the harm and reintegrating participants.
Where mediation aims for a "win/win" outcome,
conferences aim for a range of social, emotional and
behavioural outcomes for the whole community
affected by the incident. ■

Chapter 6

Conference follow-up

There are two types of follow-up that will assist the process of repair and healing.

Informal

This takes the form of a brief phone call or visit to key conference participants, perhaps in the evening after the conference or the next day. The purpose of this phone call is threefold. Firstly, it will let those participants know that the school is concerned with their welfare, especially if they had been particularly affected by the incident, or if the conference was an emotional event. And it gives people an opportunity to make further meaning of what they had experienced and will give you a sense of any unfinished business.

It will also be a valuable source of feedback about the process and your facilitation. Consider using a feedback sheet for participant comments (see Appendix). This may also serve to influence reluctant administrators.

Formal

This follow-up is in relation to compliance with the agreement. Generally speaking, the monitoring of the terms is the task of someone who has been identified and named in the agreement, rather than you as facilitator. This step is crucial in reassuring the people involved that the certainty of follow through is a priority and that every assistance is given to the wrongdoer to comply with the agreement. According to formal evaluations of school conferences and conferences in other jurisdictions, there is a very high rate of compliance with agreements. In the rare event that a wrongdoer does not appear to have complied, it is worthwhile investigating the reasons why, so that you can offer further support, or even, in an extreme case, reconvene some of the original participants for another, smaller conference.

Your responsibility with respect to the agreement is really to ensure that someone is monitoring it . ■

Chapter 7

Looking after yourself

Facilitating a conference is not for the faint hearted. It takes a firm commitment to the ideals of the restorative philosophy, appropriate skills and impeccable preparation. At all stages of the conference, where it is humanly possible, work with a colleague who understands the process. Together, you can plan the technical points – who to invite, how to seat them, what's likely to happen in the conference and how best to manage that.

Obviously, if you are co-facilitating, this assistance will be assumed, and your colleague will be able to give you valuable feedback about your performance.

But working with a colleague after the conference is every bit as important. Do not underestimate how exhausting a conference can be, even when the outcomes are all positive. It's an exacting job, and it will take a toll on your physical and emotional energy.

Plan to debrief with a colleague afterwards, even if it has to be by phone or email. Useful questions might include:

"What happened? How did it go?"

"Did it unfold in the way you expected?"

"Did people behave as you expected?"

"Do you think participants were satisfied with the process and outcomes?"

"Was there anything you discovered that you were unaware of before the conference?"

"Was the preparation adequate?"

"How did you perform? What bits were easy/hard? What do you need to work on?"

"What would you have done differently?"

"How do you feel now?"

Your toughest challenge will probably be working in a school where there is a punitive approach to managing behaviour, and you cannot influence decision-making to the extent that a deputy principal or principal is prepared to consider an alternative approach to a particular incident. Networking with other like-minded colleagues, then, will be essential for you to maintain your faith and convictions, as well as your skills. Take the time to attend network meetings and take advantage of every opportunity to enhance and maintain your skills and to keep your courage topped up. ■

Chapter 8

What if?

What if the facts of the incident don't agree and the stories are confusing?

You must be as certain as possible of the circumstances before facilitating the conference. If the admissions by the wrongdoers and the stories of the victims are inconsistent and muddy, then more work needs to be done by speaking to others who may be able to shed some light on what happened. The main issue here is that the confusion of stories will become evident in the conference and time will be wasted trying to establish the facts with possible accusations about lying – all of which are not helpful. Exact details do not need to match but who was responsible for what needs to be understood. If people generally agree that harm was done, and that harm can be explored, that may be sufficient.

What if one or more wrongdoers refuse to attend the conference?

Although this is a rare event, if one of the wrongdoers refuses the attend, s/he should be managed by the school in a different way. Remember, the conference is incident-based, not wrongdoer-centred, and if you choose not to go ahead with the conference, then you need to think about how best to meet the needs of the community of people who have been affected by the behaviour. Talk through the issues with someone who understands the philosophy and the risks. You can go ahead with the conference if one or more wrongdoers agree to participate.

What if the victim does not want to attend?

Many victims are reluctant to attend initially. By carefully painting a picture of what the conference process will look like and the role they will have, chances are they will agree to attend. Your sales pitch needs to include what they might get out of the conference: Why did it happen to me? Are they sorry for what they did to me? Do they understand the harm they have caused? And, will it happen to me again? Victims often have concerns about being 'attacked' again by the wrongdoer/s and can be so distressed that they cannot be in the same room as the wrongdoer. The role of the victim's supporters needs to be visited so that victims can feel secure. And there is of course the agreement. What does the victim want to see happen? In rare cases, if the victim is simply too frightened to attend, s/he can write a letter to the wrongdoer to be read out during the conference, or they can choose someone to represent them (an elder brother, colleague or close friend).

But doesn't putting the bully and the victim in the same room revictimise the victim?

Victims of bullying mostly want to be left alone, to be safe again and to have an answer to the question "why me?" They are also rightly fearful that if they speak up in a conference, they will invite retaliation for having done so and for having "dobbed" in the first place. The enormous amount of research about bullying clearly indicates that punishment does not change bullying behaviour, so what options do we have to ensure the safety of the victim and stop the behaviour? A restorative approach is then really the only solution. Your job in the preparation phase of the conference is to reassure the victim and his/her parents that:

- they will not be further harmed
- the conference is designed to give people a chance to tell their stories of fear, reluctance to come to school, loss of self-confidence and withdrawal
- the parents of the bully need to hear this and talk about their own issues and concerns
- compliance with any agreement reached is more likely to occur when wrongdoer supporters are part of the negotiations
- you, as facilitator, will manage the process so it doesn't get out of hand
- someone will be monitoring the situation very carefully
- if they are still too fearful to attend, their interests can be represented by their parents or an older sibling

What if the parent/s of the victim or the wrongdoer refuse to attend or cannot make it?

Despite your best efforts the parent may still not attend to support their son or daughter. You will need to find another significant person to support the victim or wrongdoer. This could be a relative, aunt or uncle, sports coach, teacher or peers. Do your best to convince the parents to attend as they are most important to the transformative process.

Restorative Practices in Schools

If they refuse you would need to contact them after the conference to talk about what happened, the terms of the agreement and any strategies that have been designed to support their son or daughter.

What if the victim and family want the incident to be formally handled by the police or courts?

Often this demand is driven by anger and distress caused by the incident. It is important to detail how the conference may provide the opportunity to hear from the wrongdoer and to understand the motivation behind the incident. The victims and their families need to know that they can participate in the conference and if not satisfied, refer the matter to the police or civil courts. The conference does not bind people to the agreement or exclude other sanctions if they are not satisfied. In our experience, further action is extremely rare.

What if there are no apparent victims?

Some problem behaviours appear to have no primary victims. Some seem to be offences only against property. Examples of these include student involvement with illicit substances, truancy, graffiti on school structures and destruction of school property. Remember that conferences are incident-based rather than wrongdoer and victim based. You will be inviting the community who have been affected by the behaviour. We just need a simple shift in our thinking to identify who are the victims. They may be people significant to the wrongdoer, people responsible for an area of school operations, cleaners, emergency services etc. There is always someone who has been affected.

What about drugs?

Illicit drug-related offences will need to be dealt with in accordance with state policy and legislation. In most instances, it is required that school officials report the matter to the police. Police will exercise their judgement about how they will deal with the incident, perhaps with a caution. Be aware that, whatever they decide, there are relationships that still need mending, lessons to be learnt, and support for the wrongdoer to be organised. In our experience, drug offences cause strong emotional responses and debate in the school community. The best forum for this debate to play out with key affected parties is the conference. If the school is lucky enough to have a school-based police officer, who is also a trained facilitator, they might be the facilitator of choice in this instance.

Some schools have a zero tolerance policy on illicit drugs. Exclusion is automatic. The wrongdoer is "cleansed" from the school population in the blink of an eye. The lost opportunities in choosing to deal with a problem of this sort in this way are endless. A school needs to consider how they can, on the one hand, choose to deal with certain sorts of incident in one way (restoratively) and in complete contrast, isolate and stigmatise wrongdoers, and fail to deal with the needs of the affected community on the other, with such a policy.

Some wrongdoers may argue that their drug-related behaviour is only affecting themselves. A conference may be a very powerful process to demonstrate to the wrongdoer who else has been affected and in what ways. Hopefully the conference also has the potential to change drug-related behaviour through highlighting the harm caused to relationships.

What if parents object to their son or daughter participating?

You may need to do some homework here. Have the parents been fully informed of the process? Perhaps they need to participate as well. Think of why the normal, protective parent would object. Remember the fundamental philosophy of restorative justice – harm to people and relationships creates obligations and liabilities. Do they understand the seriousness and circumstances of the incident? Are they aware of the alternatives if their child does not attend the conference? Does this situation "push buttons" for them about some injustice that has happened to them in the past? You may need to reassure them that this process is likely to be very different.

Can the teacher who discovered the wrongdoers, or who is investigating the incident, facilitate the conference?

Generally, it not a good idea, because they will not be able, as facilitator, to talk about what they thought or felt, or take part in reaching agreement. It would be much more effective to have them as participants in the conference. A teacher should not facilitate if they have any victim status; for example if some of the teacher's property was damaged, the teacher was verbally/physically abused by the wrongdoer(s), or even threatened in some minor way by the wrongdoer(s). In a nutshell, if the teacher is a member of the community who has been harmed by the incident, then they should not facilitate the conference. Having said that, there will be circumstances (for example, on school camp) which will mean no one else is available to facilitate an "on the spot" conference. In that case, declare your interests during the conference by saying:

"I'm just going to take my facilitator's hat off for a moment ..."

What if an advocate does not want the wrongdoer or victim to participate in the conference?

It is not unusual for a young person's advocate to question the conference process. This may depend on the young person's status and who they identify with in terms of race, religion, ethnicity etc. Some advocates may feel that the young person will be participating unrepresented, or may say something that will be incriminating during the conference. It will be important to take the time to explain the conference process to the advocate, particularly about the freedom to leave the conference at any stage and the nature of the final agreement, both legally and morally. To encourage participation it may be useful to talk about what will (or won't) be achieved if other sanctions are put in place (expulsion, police, court etc). It is acceptable to invite the advocate to the conference as an observer. As an observer they do not participate in the circle, nor do they speak.

What if a participant arrives at the conference with a legal representative?

Insist that the representative stay only as an observer. It may be necessary to inform them that anything their client says in the conference is not admissible in any other jurisdiction. They may also leave the conference at any time with their client. The representative will then need to understand that if the wrongdoer leaves, the matter will be handled differently by the school. From our experience this would be an extremely rare event. Lawyers, however, do need to understand that you, as facilitator, are in charge, and this process is part of the regular school "disciplinary" process after all!

What if the wrongdoer/s do not attend the conference on the day?

The conference should not go ahead. Other sanctions may need to be applied by the school. It may be appropriate to reconvene the conference if the wrongdoer has a genuine excuse for not attending. As facilitator, you may know the wrongdoer's story well, but do not try to replace the wrongdoer by telling their version of events, or allowing a supporter to do so. This will lead to other parties becoming incensed and more harm is likely to be caused.

What if the conference begins and a participant arrives late?

Here you will need to use very good judgement. It may be best to quickly introduce the person and continue with the conference. Depending on how far the conference has proceeded, it may be more appropriate to have them sit outside the circle and not participate. You will need to weigh up having one upset person compared to the rest being upset. If their attendance is crucial for the success of the conference process, consider delaying the start time. Think of their role in the conference to help with your decision.

What if someone turns up drunk or otherwise under the influence?

If the person is to play a significant role in the conference, or you judge there is a risk of serious disruption, reconvene the conference on another day. Ask the principal to make contact with that person later to discuss the issues around participation. If the person is not an essential participant, ask them to leave.

What if the wrongdoer/s admit to new wrongdoings during the conference?

Use your judgement. If the offences were not serious you can continue and deal with them after the conference by way of another conference or in other restorative ways. If they are of a serious nature you may need to stop the conference for a short time, make arrangements with the wrongdoer to manage these problem behaviours later and then reconvene the conference with an explanation of the circumstances and decisions to all participants.

What if the wrongdoer/s show apparent contempt by smiling, laughing, or inappropriate body language?

Often this behaviour demonstrates fear, shyness or a lack of social skills and maturity. You will need to intervene if the victims respond angrily to the behaviour. Often the best interventions are those from the supporters of the wrongdoer. Ask a significant supporter to disapprove of the behaviour.

What if there is a difference in the numbers of victims or wrongdoers or their supporters?

From our experience, having an imbalance in numbers of victims or wrongdoers and/or their supporters is not a problem if you prepare participants carefully. Choose appropriately sensible supporters who can help victims and wrongdoers feel safe. You must emphasise that the purpose of the conference is to repair the harm done, not cause more, and that you will be vigilant in ensuring this is so.

If a victim or wrongdoer discloses previously unknown incidents of sexual or physical abuse, should the conference be stopped?

Not necessarily. Your next move will depend on the circumstances and ages of those involved. If the perpetrator of the offence is a participant, depending on their age, a complete end to the conference may be the best course of action. Formal reporting to relevant authorities may be mandated. On the other hand, if the perpetrator is not present, and the age difference and relationship will not divert the focus of the conference, plan to continue. Firstly, acknowledge what has been said and provide an opportunity to address this after the conference.

Is it OK to go back over some parts of the script?

Certainly, if it assists participants to further understand the motivation and background to the incident, and assists in deeper exploration of the harm. An example would be if reaching agreement is being impeded by an unresolved issue for one or more participants. Another instance might be if young wrongdoers have little ability to reflect upon their behaviour and/or might not be able to "read the play" when the time comes for an apology. Enlist the assistance of their supporters by asking:

"Is there any way you can help him understand what harm has been done?"

What if we know that there is a history of violence in the family? Will this put the wrongdoer at risk?

It is far less likely that a wrongdoer will be at risk of violence as a result of the conference.

Since the student is already "in trouble", the risk of violence at home is probably greater if a conference is not used to resolve the difficulties. The healing power of the conference makes it a far more effective forum for dealing with the strong emotions that result in violent behaviour. If you have ongoing concerns about the safety of the young wrongdoer, make sure someone close to the family is invited to offer support and protection to the family in the days and weeks after the conference.

Do people lose control and become violent in the conference?

The worst that is likely to happen during a conference is that someone will become so angry that they will feel that they have to leave the room. In this case, send one of the participants (the counsellor or deputy principal) outside with them, to calm them and bring them back into the process.

What if the victims make unreasonable demands to repair the harm?

This simple question requires a detailed response. Management of the agreement will go smoothly if the facilitator has done their job of following the script with the correct sequence of questioning and listened carefully for indications that an issue would benefit from further exploration. In matters of property damage, requests for material reparation will be usual and quite fair. But in matters of harm to people, calls for material rather than symbolic reparation may demonstrate that some key issues have been missed or that the conference process has been somehow skewed. Some explanations may be:

- The wrongdoer has not told enough of their story to paint enough of a picture of their motivation or circumstances
- The wrongdoer is not showing signs of genuine remorse
- A participant may not be able to read others' emotions accurately
- The harm caused has not been explored sufficiently
- The conference process has not been able to help some deal with their underlying emotions
- Preparation for the conference has been superficial
- The right people are not participating in the conference
- The facilitator is showing bias or is taking the moral high ground
- The timing of the conference is inappropriate

You may need to revisit appropriate parts of the script. You could hand the challenge over to the group by saying something like:

"We seem to be stuck here. ... is asking for something that some of you feel is unfair. What are the issues that we're not seeing? Does anyone have any ideas about how we might reach consensus?"

What if the wrongdoer refuses to abide by the agreement?

It is rare that compliance with the agreement is a problem as a result of the wrongdoer simply refusing to do what was asked of him/her. It is more likely that there has been some kind of technical problem and simple problem-solving and support will assist them in meeting their obligations. If all else fails, reconvene a smaller conference, with some of the key people present (wrongdoer, his/her parents, deputy principal, other supporters) to explore the obstacles to compliance and plan to meet the obligations inherent in the agreement. ■

Appendix

Preparation checklist

Before the conference

- [ ] Facts have been clarified with investigator and key people

- [ ] All participants have been contacted and 'prepared' for the conference

- [ ] Time has been spent considering what the possible dynamics of the conference may be like

- [ ] Participants have adequate transport to get to and from the conference

- [ ] Child minding is arranged if necessary

- [ ] The venue is booked and cleaners, security and grounds people are aware

- [ ] The room is organised according to the seating plan and room temperature is comfortable

- [ ] Paperwork for the conference is prepared (script, seating plan, agreement, case notes, evaluation sheet)

- [ ] Food and drink and tissues are ready in the room

- [ ] Final phone calls made to check if people can still attend and final questions answered

- [ ] Meeting and greeting place is organised and appropriate 'separation' areas planned

After the conference

- [ ] Copy of the agreement handed out or sent to each participant

- [ ] Contact with participants made to check on their wellbeing and conference outcomes

- [ ] Conference evaluation completed for school records and student files

- [ ] De-brief with a colleague

Restorative Practices in Schools

Conference script

1. Introduction

Welcome. As you know, my name is ...... , and I will be coordinating this conference. Before the conference begins, I would like to introduce everybody briefl y and indicate their reasons for being here.

(Another version might look like this:

I want to thank everybody for being here today. Some of you are missing out on your lunchtime/meeting time/sport practice/ time with your family/planning other school activities. Before we start I want to go around the group and explain why people are here today.)

The introductions are usually performed in order around the circle.

At this stage, I would like to thank you all for making the effort to attend. This is a diffi cult (and /or complicated/sensitive) **matter, and your participation here will help us deal with it.**

The conference will focus on the incident (.........) **which happened (.........), involving** (wrongdoer's and victim's names).

It's important to understand that we will focus on what (wrongdoer's name) **did and how his/her behaviour has affected others. We are not here to decide whether** (wrongdoer's name) **is a good or bad person. We want to explore how people have been affected, and see whether we can begin to repair the harm that has been done.**

(Alternatively:

*We are all here today to talk about what happened.......
when......who........ We are not going to talk about ....,
.........., and .... as good or bad people. We are only
going to talk about what they did. Today we need to fi nd
out what happened and why, and what harm has been
caused by this incident. All of us here today will help to
repair the harm and to make an agreement that will
make sure that this does not happen again. When this
agreement is reached, it will be the end of this conference.
If ...., ... and ..... stick to the agreement, the school will
do nothing more. You will be all given a chance to tell
your story. Everyone in turn will have a chance to be
heard. This means that we will be here for about 2 hours.
Is that OK?)*

To wrongdoer/s:

you have admitted your involvement in the incident. If at any stage during the conference you no longer wish to participate, you are free to leave – but if you choose to do so, the matter will be dealt with differently. This matter will be fi nished when this conference is over and you have completed what people ask you to do to repair the harm. Is that clear?

(Alternatively:

You can leave the conference any time you like, but if you do you need to know that what you did will be handled differently by the school. Do you understand this?)

2. Telling the story

Wrongdoer(s):

- **............, to help us understand what harm has been done and who has been affected by this incident, could you start by telling us what happened?**
- **How did you come to be involved?**
- **What were you thinking at the time?**

(Or

- *What were you hoping would happen?*
- *What were you expecting would happen?*
- *What was the purpose of doing that?*
- *What was going on in your head at the time?*
- *What made you decide to do that?*
- **What have you thought about since?**

(Or

- *What have you thought about since this has all happened?)*
- **Who do you think has been affected by your actions?**
- **In what way?**

3. Exploring the harm

Victim(s):

- **What did you think at the time?**
- **What have you thought about since?**
- **How has this incident affected you?**
- **How did your family and friends react when they heard about the incident?**
- **What has been the worst of it for you?**

Or

- **What are the main issues here for you?**

Victim supporters:

- What did you think when you heard about the incident?
- How do you feel about what has happened?
- What has happened since?
- What changes have you seen in your son/daughter?

Or

- What changes have you seen in your colleague?
- As …'s parent/friend/colleague, what has been the hardest for you?

Or

- What are the main issues here for you? What has been the worst of it for you?

Wrongdoer supporters:

- It must be difficult for you to hear this.
- What did you think when you heard?
- How do you feel about what has happened?
- What has happened since?
- How has it affected you?
- In the wake of what's happened, how are things at home/between you all?
- What has been the worst of it?

4. Acknowledgement and apology

Wrongdoer:

Now that you've heard from everybody about how they've been affected by what you've done, is there anything you want to say to ……… (the victim), **or anyone else here? Is there something that you could say which might begin to make things right?**

If necessary:

Is there something … (victim, parents, teacher, etc), **needs to hear from you right now?**

5. Agreement

To the victim first and then the victim supporters:

- What do you want to see happen as a result of the conference/meeting today (or to repair the harm)?

Allow plenty of time for discussion as suggestions are tabled.

To wrongdoer *and* wrongdoer supporters:

- Does that seem fair?

It is also useful to ask the wrongdoer and his/her supporters for their ideas about how to make amends:

- Is there something that you would like to see happen that might help?

To all conference participants:

- Who will be responsible for supervising the terms of the agreement?
- How would you all like to be kept in the loop?

Let me just summarise what you have agreed upon.

You read the list of actions and get final agreement to commit it to paper.

6. Closing the conference

To the whole group:

I will now record the agreement that's been reached here. This will formally close the matter, subject to completion of the agreement. You will each be asked to sign it and you will be given a copy before you leave.

Is there anything else anyone wants to say?

Leave a little time for people to compose their thoughts, then say:

You have all worked hard to resolve this incident and the agreement you have reached should go a long way towards repairing the harm that has been done.

While I write down the agreement, which I will ask you all to sign before you leave, please enjoy the refreshments we have provided for you.

Conference agreement

The following agreement was reached at a community conference that took place at:

	Date:	/ /

and was facilitated by:

It was agreed that:

The agreement will be monitored by [ ] and follow-up will occur:

Names of participants: Signatures:

Conference evaluation sheet

Please complete this evaluation about the conference in which you have just participated. It will give us some feedback about the process and show us how we might improve it.

1.   Please circle your role in the conference:

Student   Teacher   School Management

Parent/Carer   Supporter   Other

2.   On a scale of 1–5 what was the conference like for you? (please circle)

1 = Very good   2 = Good   3 = OK   4 = Not so good   5 = Very poor

3.   Was the conference a fair way to deal with this incident/situation?

4.   Were you able to say all you wanted to say?

5.   Was it helpful to hear other people's stories?

6.   Were you satisfied with the agreement at the end of the conference?

7.   Do you think the agreement will work?

8.   Do you think things will change for you in the future as a result of the conference?

9.   Do you think this conferencing process is a good way to sort out problems?

10.   Is there anything else you would like to say about the conference?

Information for community conference participants

What is a community conference?

A community conference is a meeting of the community of people affected by an incident of serious harm in the school or community setting. The conference provides a forum in which wrongdoers, those harmed and their respective supporters can seek ways to repair the damage caused by the incident or situation, and minimise further harm.

A conference gives wrongdoers an opportunity to understand the impact of their behaviour on other people, themselves and the wider community in the school and beyond. It gives wrongdoers a chance to atone for their actions. A conference gives those harmed the opportunity to explain how they have been affected and to become involved in negotiating how to repair the harm.

Who attends a community conference?

A conference usually involves the following people:

- The wrongdoer and their supporters
- Those harmed and their supporters
- The conference facilitator (an experienced and trained person)
- The school officer who investigated the incident
- Other school and/or community personnel if appropriate

What happens during a community conference?

Participants listen to the stories of what happened so they have a clear understanding of the impact of the behaviour on everyone present. The damage may be physical or emotional. They then decide what needs to be done to repair the damage and minimise further harm. An agreement is reached which is recorded and signed by key people present. These people are given a copy of the agreement. Follow-up occurs at an agreed time.

What are the outcomes of a conference?

The main outcome of a conference is the written agreement described above. The terms of the agreement may include anything from an apology and assurances that the behaviour will not occur again, to community service work around the school or elswhere, repayment of money (if appropriate), repair of any physical damage to property, and undertakings by the student or family to access appropriate support. The outcomes are limited only by the group's imagination and its ability to ensure compliance with the terms of the agreement. The process is designed to achieve maximum satisfaction for all those who participate.

How long does a community conference take?

This will depend on the circumstances and complexity of the situation and the number of people involved and willing to participate. The time taken to prepare for the conference is totally dependent on these factors, with the conference itself taking, on average, one and a half to two hours. Considering the time usually taken to deal with such incidents, this is a reasonable investment of time for the school or community.

What are the advantages of this approach?

Those harmed get the opportunity to have their say in a safe forum, both about how they were affected and what they want to see happen to repair the harm. Family and other supporters also get to talk about what has happened to them as a result of the incident, and they take part in deciding what needs to be done. The wrongdoer is confronted, often for the first time, with how their behaviour has affected others, including their own families. They take responsibility for their behaviour and are not allowed to walk away from the community of people they have hurt. Relationships are strengthened and extended, and they are given the opportunity to find a way to be accepted back into the community. Everyone at the conference learns from the experience and often there are dramatic behaviour changes.

Where this process is used to solve high level conflict or other relationship difficulties, bringing the community of people together in this way to problem-solve gives those involved insights which are often not possible with other approaches, and can also unite the community of people affected. Peace is a possibility.

Recommended reading

There has been so much written about restorative justice and psychological theory that explains its effectiveness – texts, conference papers, research – that a beginner could be overwhelmed. What we recommend below is a starting point. Each of these will lead you elsewhere. Do read more. It will increase your overall understanding of the field and ultimately, your practice.

Texts

▩ *Crime, Shame and Reintegration.* 1989. Braithwaite, J., Cambridge University Press.

▩ *Shame and Pride: Affect, sex, and the birth of self.* 1992. Nathanson, D.L., New York, W.W. Norton.

▩ *Restorative Justice and Civil Society.* 2001. Ed Strang, H. and Braithwaite, J., Cambridge University Press.

▩ *Calling the Circle – The First and Future Culture.* 1994. Baldwin, C., New York, Bantam Books.

▩ *The Little Book of Restorative Justice.* 2004. Zehr, H., Mika, H., Sage Publications.

Articles

▩ The Name of the Game is Shame. Nathanson, D.L. *www.tomkins.org*

▩ A Conversation with Don Nathanson, *behavior.net/column/nathanson/*

▩ Fundamental Concepts of Restorative Justice. Zehr, H., Mika, H. *ojp.usdoj.gov/nij/publications/rest-just/ch1/fundamental.html*

Available from Incentive Publishing

▩ *Beyond Zero Tolerance: Restorative Practices in Schools* DVD. 2002–3. International Institute for Restorative Practices.

▩ *Conferencing Handbook.* 1999. O'Connell, T., Wachtel, B. and Wachtel, T.

▩ *Face to Face* DVD. 2003. Somerset Youth Offending Team.

▩ *Introducing Restorative Justice* DVD. 2005. Milton Keynes Psychological Service.

▩ *Just Schools: A Whole School Approach to Restorative Justice.* 2003. Hopkins, B.

▩ *Roundtable Discussion 1* DVD. International Institute for Restorative Practices.

▩ *Roundtable Discussion 2* DVD. International Institute for Restorative Practices.

▩ *Restorative Practices and Bullying: Rethinking Behaviour Management.* 2008. Thorsborne, M. and Vinegrad, D.

▩ *Restorative Practices in Classrooms: Rethinking Behaviour Management.* 2008. Thorsborne, M. and Vinegrad, D.

▩ *Six Conferences* DVD, International Institute for Restorative Practices.

Other useful web addresses

▩ *iirp.org/library.php*

▩ *thorsborne.com.au*

▩ *tribes.com*

Applying conferencing across the school setting

Introduction

A school committed to preventative behaviour management will seek ways to promote pro-social behaviours amongst the student population. In practise, many schools teach the values around behaviours by default, through the example of school staff and their conduct around the school. This hidden curriculum can work positively where teachers practise what they preach. This means, in a restorative school, using restorative dialogue with students and incorporating reintegrative and transformative interventions in the classroom. Some of these may include Individual, Small and Medium-size group conferences and classroom conferences. In these instances, parents do not attend, although they may be informed beforehand and afterwards if the matter is serious enough.

The conference process, usually suggested for behaviours and incidents which would normally attract suspension and/or exclusion, has much to offer behaviour management across the wider school community. Whether classroom, playground, school excursion, major incident or minor infringement, conferencing can appropriately respond to and resolve harmful behaviour. Schools that use conferences to address major incidents comment that the script language and process gradually filter through the school environment. Classroom teachers begin to 'walk the talk'. The language and intent of conferencing can be incorporated as a student behaviour management process for all schools from early childhood to tertiary institutions.

Many schools have established codes of conduct and behaviour management practices based on rights and responsibilities, with an ideal outcome that students will be taught and encouraged to own their behaviour. Restorative approaches have the potential to achieve these outcomes. Students, when given the opportunity to reflect on how their behaviour has impacted on others, begin to understand their own actions and are more likely to take responsibility for them. The use of conferencing as a major restorative intervention provides the interpersonal and disciplinary link between proactive student management policies and the life of the classroom and playground.

The benefit for schools in the long term is that the staff and student population undergo fundamental behaviour and culture change. The focus on a more open and transformative dialogue impacts positively on the daily operations of the school. Conferencing methods can be applied in a range of ways to provide a restorative intervention with individual students, small groups and classes and whole year groups.

The following scenarios are designed to give you examples of how the conferencing script and process can be used to manage individual, small and medium-size group conferences. They are not prescriptive, merely included to show you that you can adapt the process for any situation that is disciplinary in nature. These conferences are almost instantaneous and are facilitated 'on the spot'. There is no pre-conference preparation. There are only slight changes to the script and to the order of questioning. As you become more familiar with the language and script, so will your students. You may begin to hear students using the language amongst themselves. The teacher in these "on the spot" conferences may play multiple roles: facilitator one minute, those harmed or supporter the next.

Individual conference: one student

In the following scenarios an individual conference is used as a brief intervention in the playground, classroom and corridors. There may have been simple breaches of rules: late to class, failure to bring class materials, refusing to share the tasks in group work, swearing, harassment and bullying at student lockers, exclusion of others. These individual conferences (a "restorative conversation") can replace those difficult teacher–student interactions that often encourage secondary behaviours because the teacher feels obliged to address the student's attitude. This kind of behaviour is often seen by children and adolescents as a moot point:

"I wasn't hurting anyone", "I gave it back, and anyway they did that to me last time", "I finished my work and you said we can do what we like", "They always sit next to me, she smells and won't stop looking at my work".

Scenario 1: Late to class

Sam is late to class, again. The teacher allows Sam to join the class with a calm "Sam, please sit down quickly and begin the work". When the class is on task or at the end of the lesson the teacher finds a suitable place in the classroom and conducts an individual conference with Sam: The teacher establishes equal terms with Sam: facing each other with heads at the same height (respect and dignity rather than superiority and humiliation before peers).

"Sam, we need to talk about you being late to class."

The structure of these questions is important, don't rush them. The question above is a statement about being late, there is no room for debate or denial. You have stated the fact.

(Saying "Sam, we need to talk about your behaviour" or "Sam, why were you late?" will go nowhere for both of you.)

"Sam, what were you thinking/feeling about when you were coming to our class late?"

This question asks for the background to the incident. You need to listen. This will tell you if Sam has poor organisational or decision-making abilities. Be prepared though to hear "Your class is boring, I didn't want to come". Do not rise to the bait! Simply ask:

"What have you thought about since getting to class?"

This question may give you a picture of how Sam feels. Whether he is remorseful, fearful of being punished, his place in the class, attachment to the school. Some students will be keen to make amends whilst others will be expecting the school to 'do it to them' once again.

"When you come late to class who is affected by your behaviour?"

You may need to lead the student through this reflective question, but be careful not to moralise. Ask leading questions like "How about the group you have been working on the project with?", or "How does it affect me, what am I doing right now, what should I be doing?" This is an opportunity for the student to learn about social responsibility. The teacher may have 'those harmed' status here and

then move quickly to reintegrate the wrongdoer. "Sam, you are a terrific student and I enjoy your participation in this class. Coming late is pretty silly stuff that is spoiling your good work."

"How is your work group and the rest of the class affected when you come late?"

This is mixed in with the above question to explore the depth of the harm. This question leaves the trivial, wrongful behaviour behind and investigates if the student is connected to the class, whether they have insight into their behaviour and if there is an opportunity to learn from this incident.

"How has this affected/harmed you?"

Sam is asked to own his behaviour and its impact on himself.

"What do you need to do to fix things?"

Here is the agreement stage and the chance to make amends and to formulate plans for the future.

"What can I do to help you?"

The teacher begins to share the accountability. Another glimpse into the world of the student may be available as the teacher 'patches up' the relationship with this important offer.

This most basic application of the conference script builds restorative language and proactive teacher behaviour into the classroom. The above dialogue should take only 1–2 minutes. How long does a detention or a notation in the teacher's book take? And, what is the effect of a punitive approach on the student and on your relationship with them?

The above process is applied with respect and dignity. The student is not berated or belittled in front of their peers. There is no power play, and the teacher and student explore the incident in a controlled, calm manner. The opening questions are non-judgemental and the student hopefully feels that the teacher is listening to them (one of the common student complaints about teachers: they do not listen). The script blends nicely with other teacher micro skills as the responsibility for the behaviour is placed firmly with the student. The use of the script to is to focus on a conscience-building exercise with the student so that they may begin to understand their own motivation and reflect on how their behaviour impacts on others.

Small to medium-size group conference

Scenario 1: The missing wallet

Students are participating in group work, moving freely around the classroom. Towards the end of the lesson a student, in an agitated manner, informs the teacher that their wallet has been taken from their jacket which was on the desk. The teacher was about to stop the class to conduct a search when the victim calls out that they have found their wallet on a chair. The victim also calls out "Nicky took it". Nicky then calls out to the victim that it was "just a joke, I was only mucking around". The teacher quickly tells the victim and wrongdoer to remain behind at the end of the class so that "we can get it sorted out". The teacher keeps an eye on both students until the end of the lesson. The class have left and the conference begins.

To the wrongdoer:

"Nicky, Ashley, we need to sort out the incident with the wallet."

Teacher sits down with both students in a triangle.

"Nicky, what were you thinking about when you took the wallet?"

"What have you thought about since it happened?"

"Who has been affected by what you did? In what ways have they been affected?"

To the victim:

"How did you feel when you noticed your wallet missing?"

"What was the worst thing about it?"

To the wrongdoer:

"What needs to be done/said to fix things?"

To the victim:

"Is there anything else that you would like to see happen?"

To wrongdoer and victim:

"Is this the end of the matter?"

"This is what we have agreed on ...."

This small group conference should take only several minutes. The alternative to this in a punitive setting could have been a heated argument with the wrongdoer who was 'playing a joke' yet behaved inappropriately. A lecture about personal property, theft and practical jokes may have had little impact on the wrongdoer, and the victim may have wanted to 'even the score' after class.

Scenario 3: Rumours in the playground

Several students approach a duty teacher out in the playground. They report that two other students have been spreading rumours about their mothers. They are saying that their mothers are 'povos' (very poor) and they smell because they don't wash. The teacher asks the students what they would like done to sort out the harassment. The teacher offers a range of options including assistance from the principal and year level manager, suspension, detention, or just talking to them about it.

The students choose the latter. The teacher accompanies the victims to seek out the wrongdoers in the playground. When found, the conference begins. The teacher arranges the students in a circle right there in the playground but away from others. On one side are the two victims and their two supporters/witnesses and on the other side are both wrongdoers.

"Girls, these people have made a formal report of verbal harassment. They were given a choice of working it out by suspensions, reporting it to the principal, detentions or by meeting with you now, to sort it out. They chose this, to meet and talk about it. Do you want to get it sorted out?"

"Let's begin by asking the girls what happened, what their report is about."

To the wrongdoers:

"Is that what happened?"

"What were you thinking at the time?"

"What are you thinking about now, since we have started talking?"

"Who has been affected by what you did/said? How do you think they feel?"

To the victims:

"How do you feel about what they were saying?"

Restorative Practices in Schools

To the supporters:

"How did you feel when you heard what was said?"

To the wrongdoers:

"What can you do to sort this out? What needs to be done?"

"What else can we do to make sure that this does not happen again?"

To the victims:

"Do you accept their apology? What else needs to be done?"

Classroom conferences – whole of class

Refer to our manual *Restorative Practices in Classrooms*.

Case studies

The following three cases were contributed by the co-author, David Vinegrad, who facilitated these conferences while working in student welfare and teaching in high schools in Tasmania and Victoria, Australia. *See "About this Manual" for his contact details.*

The pub

The following incident was resolved and managed by the community conference process.

Of significance is the role played by this school in a community that was the last broad acre housing commission development implemented in Tasmania, which, at one point in time, was famous for having the worst levels of community health in Australia.

During a usual school day several students truanted and returned to the school intoxicated. These students disrupted many classes, assaulted a male teacher and then left the school grounds followed by a trail of administrators and onlookers. The school was keen to limit the damage from this incident and to sort it out with the best interests of all in mind.

The list of defined "wrongdoers" for this conference included a female student who was responsible for purchasing the alcohol, two male and one female student who consumed the alcohol and the manager of the hotel who was liable for selling the alcohol. Of interest was the manager of the hotel who was visibly tired of the ongoing community backlash against his pub for providing alcohol to their kids. He was keen to view the school as an ally in all this trouble.

The conference was a success. The school, once again, received feedback about its boring, ad hoc and irrelevant curriculum. The offending students were reintegrated back into their school community and their parents and guardians were pleased with the process and outcomes. The male teacher was able to speak about his shock and surprise at the assault and disclosed later that he felt comfortable talking about his distress rather than keeping up his masculine front. The local pub came out of the conference with a new sense of community understanding and support. After the manager spoke about the ongoing battle with adults purchasing alcohol for youngsters, false identification cards, under-age parties around the community and difficulty obtaining staff who could follow strict guidelines,

the community gained valuable insight into just how OK the pub was. Another result of this conference was an agreement by the manager to review all the operations of the hotel with a focus on under-age drinking. In acknowledgement of the school's work the manager donated a perpetual trophy to recognise student success. The key to this conference was the wrongdoers' understanding of the impact of their behaviour on the people who worked at the pub, where previously they felt that the pub was just a place and a building.

Fires and firewater: a victimless crime?

During a normal school morning, the actions of five year 8 girls were uncovered by a student manager.

A classroom teacher had reported that a student returned from the toilets unsteady on her feet and with glazed eyes. Further investigation revealed that up to five girls had brought alcohol onto the school property on at least three separate days, and had also lit very small grass fires with paper and cigarette lighters. The background to this incident had some interesting twists and turns:

- The cigarette lighters had been purchased at local shops and the school was undecided if it was an offence to sell these to children.

- When student managers were walking the wrongdoers to an office to conduct an interview, the girls were able to pass the drink bottle full of 'grappa' to another student in the corridor. This student was then able to hide the bottle in a locker. The managers were not aware of what had occurred.

- The 'grappa' in the bottle was virtually undrinkable. It was brought to school by one of the wrongdoers from home. Her father had a backyard still and brewed up this powerful concoction. This was not uncommon for families from refugee and migrant backgrounds.

- The incident occurred over three days in broad daylight and within full view of duty teachers.

It was decided to conduct a conference to address the harm. All of the wrongdoers were seen as good students who might benefit from gaining an understanding of just who was affected. The school also felt that it could be a constructive way to include all parents in taking some responsibility for their children and what had happened.

Participants included:

- The five female wrongdoers
- Parents and carers of the wrongdoers
- An officer from the local fire brigade
- A range of school managers who each had a significant role with the wrongdoers
- The teachers who discovered the girls
- Representatives from the student council and the school executive
- Supporters for the wrongdoers and their families.

In total 32 people attended the conference. For one wrongdoer this was a chance to tell the school why she should not be expelled. The wrongdoers painted a picture of impulsive behaviour, risk taking and experimentation with adult activities. They told stories of stealing the cans and bottles of beer from home. They thought that no one would notice. Several wrongdoers became involved because they decided to help their friends hide the alcohol rather than consider the consequences of their behaviour. Some of the wrongdoers could not understand the fuss about lighting really small fires – "We were bored."

The conference facilitator asked the five wrongdoers, "Who do you think has been affected by what you have done?" Responses from the girls showed little insight into, or consideration for, the school community. The wrongdoers' body language angered some participants: "These kids were not showing any remorse, they couldn't care less!"

The fire officer told of the deep distress he had felt recently when a family member was injured by a cigarette lighter, similar to the one the girls had been using. It had exploded and caused serious burns. He also spoke of the unnecessary waste of resources and associated danger to the school when a harmless fire 'gets away' and causes major damage and harm. A teacher told of her personal dread and fear of the day when a student, crossing the busy road opposite the school, is killed by a car, especially if impaired after drinking alcohol. An administrator spoke of the harm that might result if the student was in a practical class with dangerous machinery, once again because of the effect of alcohol. Another administrator disclosed how she felt embarrassed at her perceived incompetence when other teachers heard how easily the wrongdoers handed off the bottle of alcohol in the corridor – "right under my nose, they all think I'm incompetent as a student manager."

Parents spoke of their shame, not realising that alcohol was missing, shocked that it had ended up at school, and for three days in a row. The parent responsible for brewing up the 'grappa' commented that he was responsible for the mess: "It wasn't a good example to be setting to the kids." A carer (grandmother) told teachers not to feel responsible for not catching the kids while on yard duty. "They are terrific girls, but boy can they be sneaky."

Negotiation of the agreement included how the conference would report back any outcomes to the school community. Some teachers wanted a statement to be read out at a school assembly. Parents disagreed and the participants settled on a letter written by all the wrongdoers to the school executive apologising for their behaviour. The wrongdoer who needed to explain why an expulsion should not be invoked spoke up and said that she would be responsible for the letter: "I want to show the school that I want to stay here."

Other parts of the agreement included the fire officer returning to school to show the wrongdoers a video on the dangers of cigarette lighters. The student welfare coordinator agreed to take responsibility to make sure that the video session was arranged. Several teachers offered to visit the shop and speak with the owner about working with the school to protect the students in the school, and especially about the result of selling them cigarette lighters.

After the facilitator had asked participants, "What was it like for you when you heard about what the girls had done?", he returned to the wrongdoers: "You have heard the stories from people here today. Now tell us, how has your behaviour affected them?" The five wrongdoers had learnt quickly, they responded positively and told of their surprise at how many people were disappointed with what they had done, and that many were relieved that they had not been injured by their foolish behaviour. They couldn't believe that it had come to all this.

Stones and a conference within a conference

This case study provides several insights into the flexibility that conferencing offers as compared to more formal school responses. It involves the facilitation of two conferences for the same incident with a blend of traditional and restorative responses.

The incident occurred during a lunch hour and involved a group of five boys who threw rocks and stones at other students including a larger group of twelve boys. They threw the rocks over a shed so that they would not be seen by the victims and, for that matter, the teachers on duty. The larger group of boys (victims) did not retaliate at the time and chose simply to move away from the area. The five boys (wrongdoers) then sat down on some stairs leading to a wing of classrooms. The larger group of victims then approached the five boys and other observers. Accusations began to fly, and taunting and teasing between the groups and comments including 'you were bounced on your head by your mother' and 'you were born in a brothel' resulted in a fight between two boys, one from each group. It could not be decided whether a knee to the head or an elbow to the face chipped a tooth, but that was the result.

Later in the day the sister of one of the boys in the fight approached the other 'fighter' and threatened to 'kill him' if he touched her brother again. A senior boy was also guilty of doing some 'pushing' before the fight began.

Rock throwing had been a serious issue for the school. Before this incident two mates on a school camp were throwing rocks at each other. This resulted in one being hit in the eye, and a lengthy stay in hospital with partial loss of sight in one eye. The school responded by informing the student body that future rock throwing would result in immediate suspension from school at very least. Administrators felt that liability and accountability needs were being met by sending a strong and clear message such as this to the community. The rock throwing continued and suspensions were meted out. The school did bear some responsibility as the playgrounds provided plenty of ammunition in the form of unsealed surfaces and lack of grassed areas.

The incident involving the two groups of boys was investigated by the Assistant Principal. Students' statements were collected and the picture was becoming fairly complicated and messy. Assemblies of students were called and the message was

repeated, 'Throw rocks at our school and you will be suspended. Do it again and you will be expelled from the school.'

Some student managers were concerned that the harm resulting from the incident had not been completely addressed and there was still ill feeling and resentment between the students involved. A conference for the boys involved was suggested and all agreed for it to go ahead, aiming for some specific outcomes. Some of these involved:

- sending a different sort of message to the student body about rock throwing

- teaching this core group of students about the harm that can result when rocks injure people

- what onlookers and supporters could have done differently to avoid the harm that resulted

- to work 'with' students rather than do things 'to' students.

During the pre-conference interviews the facilitator was told about an important issue with the chipped tooth. This was the second time that the same tooth had been chipped at school. The first involved the student walking into a door as it was being opened. It was a 'no fault' accident as the student was too short to be seen through the glass in the door.

The second incident left the parents asking who would pay for the damage this time. It also left them feeling and thinking some negative things about the school. The facilitator contacted the parents of the victim and offered to conduct a conference so that the dentist's bill could be resolved. Then the single mother of the other student was contacted, told of the unresolved bill and the offer of a conference. All agreed to attend.

Now to the conferences. A large conference took place with several teachers and about twenty students. Many of the student participants took responsibility as wrongdoers and at other stages in the conference identified themselves as victims. The key stages in the incident were explored and students took responsibility for their behaviour and the harm that it had caused; all offered apologies and acknowledged their mistakes. When asked 'what needs to be done to make sure that this does not happen again?', the students suggested 'Some of us should speak at a whole school assembly about this conference and who has been affected'. Another student said 'Some of us should also make up an article for the community newsletter about rock throwing'. These things subsequently happened, impressing many in the school community. The school did not impose any suspensions or detentions for any of the students, as a result of the conference. Parents were not involved and only some of the parents knew that the conference was occurring.

Which was the more difficult task, speaking at an assembly about a mistake that was made or staying at home for a few days on a school suspension?

Nine people met at the second conference held several days later. The conference introduction was explicit and very simple: 'We have come together to hear people's stories so that we can understand what happened and to then resolve the payment of the dental bill'. The conference was attended by the boys involved in the fight, their respective parents and siblings, the boys' year level managers, and the facilitator. It was important that parents heard the full admission from each student, the threats to kill,

the comments about being born in a brothel etc. These stories needed to be heard and to be given a context. Apologies and understandings were offered and relationships were repaired. A student manager present apologised for the lack of communication between school and home on the day of the incident. This was because the victim's mother was very upset about hearing of the fight and the 'tooth' when her daughter came home and said 'you will have to get his tooth fixed again'.

Both boys offered to split the bill for the tooth. Some time was spent exploring how this could be managed and the parents agreed to make contact with each other to monitor the arrangement. This conference lasted for about forty-five minutes. In that time bridges were built, issues resolved and some positive press gained for the school in the community.

Note: Some may ask why one larger conference was not conducted. It was decided not to, due to a requirement (duty of care) that all parents would have to be informed and permission gained for their son or daughter to participate in a conference with other parents attending. Consequently, an invitation for all parents, to attend would then need to be made, possibly resulting in a conference with about fifty or more participants. If the student behaviour is not grievous or would not normally immediately involve parents, then we feel that it is important to let students 'own their behaviour'.

It needs to be mentioned that the parents of the main perpetrators were informed of the first student conference and appropriate permission sought for their children to participate. It is also good practice to inform the parents of student responses and attitudes (positive or negative) during a conference for which they are not present, along with any outcomes or agreements reached.

Experience has also shown that when the process is clearly explained to students, including the role that their parents will or will not play, it significantly promotes their cooperation and participation.

Justice and school leadership (involving a whole year level)

The last candidate, a boy, rose, went to the podium and said, "Vote for me! ———, ———, ——— (names of three other boys) are gay", and sat down. The audience laughed. The principal, who was unaware of the comment, then dismissed the whole group. Later when he learned about the comment, the principal was greatly embarrassed that he might have given the impression that he supported the bullying. In addition, it was discovered that two other candidates (brothers) had offered the boy fifty dollars to make the statement. In another assembly the comment was publicly condemned and the wrongdoer subsequently suspended. But the damage had been done.

Despite the usual school response of condemnation and suspension, there was a very real possibility that this openly defiant and cynical act of bullying would lead to increased power and fear of the boys who had organised and done this thing. Also the entire Year 12 group seemed terribly weak and unwilling to confront antisocial behaviour. They had laughed, after all, when the comment was made. Further action was needed to repair the damage and address some very important issues.

Within 24 hours a process was designed that would involve all 120 students and their Care class teachers. The design was primarily informed by the principles of restorative justice and the moral development work of Laurence Kohlberg. The venue was one large room and the general format was an

alternation between whole group and small group discussion. Kohlberg's view is that moral development is best fostered in interaction with peers. For a number of compelling reasons the victims and the wrongdoers were kept separate and were invited in only at the end of the conference. The principal attended the concluding session.

As the students entered the room in the morning, they all wanted to know what the meeting was about. Within minutes I launched into a short but provocative oration focusing on the previous day's events. What sense could be made of what happened? There were speeches of high ideals: cooperation, achievement, pride. There was an act of denigration, bullying and humiliation. Both were applauded. What did this say about this group? How could this be? Was this an example of quality, of the best they had to offer?

There were some protests in response: "I didn't do anything", "This is none of my business", " We can't do anything" etc. etc.

Every student was then asked to consider and respond in a small group of about 20 students to a series of 7 questions (given one at a time). After considering each question with the help of their teachers, the whole group would reconvene to listen to each small group. The questions were:

- *What are the reasons/fears that might stop people from expressing how they really feel or felt about what happened?*

- *What do you think needs to happen so that Year 12 students feel safe in talking about this issue?*

- *Who is willing to support these safety measures?*

- *Who do you think was affected by the incident last Wednesday? How?*

- *At the time it happened or when you heard about it, what did you think/feel about what happened?*

- *What do you think/feel about the incident now that you have had time to think/reflect upon it? What are the main issues for you?*

- *What needs to happen to repair the damage and build trust?*

The process took about three hours. Not all the questions were discussed. Sometimes there were earnest small group discussions, sometimes angry protest, sometimes heartfelt disclosure of the personal experience of humiliation as a victim. Slowly things changed. One large, muscular boy, who previously protested about being there, took the microphone and addressed the whole group.

This case was provided by Isaac Williamson, School Counsellor, at a high school in Queensland, Australia.

Isaac, a long time devotee of the restorative approach and an experienced and creative facilitator, has adapted the principles and philosophy here to deal with the challenge of an incident which impacted on the whole cohort of final year students at his school.

Isaac Williamson can be contacted by email on: iwill8eq@eq.edu.au

Several years ago, the Year 12 students at our local high school assembled to hear the policy speeches by the candidates for school captain and vice captain. The candidates generally appealed to fellow students to aspire to work together, set a good example, take pride in the school and themselves and, of course, elect someone who would represent these higher ideals.

He told everyone that although he had not been bullied, he had seen bullying at school and now wanted to take a stand against it.

The last task was for each small group to compose a message to the wrongdoers, the victims, to the principal. A spokesperson read the messages out for each group. Some typical examples were:

To the victims – We support you, we are sorry, we feel for you.

To the wrongdoers – Think before you do something that may hurt somebody. You shouldn't pressure someone into doing something that's wrong

To the principal – Thanks for the trust in our maturity, thanks for caring.

One group had an additional message to any student absent on the day – "We are different now".

How much of a difference did it all make? Bullying didn't disappear, but it wasn't a big problem that year for the senior students. The wrongdoers were not elected but they did go on to graduate. The brothers have finished university and have successful military careers. Sometimes I hear from them. Other students who were more peripheral at the time commented on how someone they thought disliked them actually said hello after that meeting. But most of all I'd like to think that the comment "We are different" reflected a sense of communal growth, humanity and belonging that still continues to colour memories of that final year of school.

The following case studies have been contributed by a teacher, Donna Brunt, at a Catholic high school in Victoria, Australia. She has adapted the process in a number of creative ways to fit her circumstances. She has also designed a simple feedback instrument (see below) to evaluate the usefulness of this approach to problem solving.

Donna says:

The language used in the community conferencing process is easily transferred to a variety of contexts in the school community. It is particularly useful in conflict situations that demonstrate bullying type behaviours, as well as potential conflict situations where there may be communication breakdown.

1. Bullying/conflict: mini-conference

As a coordinator, I have had the opportunity to use the conferencing language to mediate in a number of conflict or potential conflict situations.

One of these situations was a bullying conflict between a large group of friends. The questions included:

- *Take us back to the start; tell us step by step what happened.*

- *What were you feeling/thinking at the time?*

- *What have you thought about since?*

- *Who do you think has been affected by your actions?*

- *How do you think they were affected?*

Allowing people to tell their story step by step gives them the opportunity to convey their perspective and, most importantly, it allows their opposition to see things from the other person's point of view. It was often at this point that both parties realised that they often shared the same feelings and were reacting to misunderstanding and/or misinformation. In a few incidents, students learned that they had been manipulated by peers, but they did not feel "blamed" as they shared their story. They were much more willing to take responsibility for their actions, apologising and coming up with strategies to avoid further conflict in the future. The results have been very positive and the students felt surprised about how effective "simply" talking things through could be. One particular group of students commented to me "you've done this before", and the students were further encouraged when I spoke to them about the conferencing training I had undertaken; it seemed to reinforce their confidence in the process.

2. Student–teacher: mini-conference

The conferencing process was also used in a mediation between a student and teacher who were not communicating effectively.

The student was struggling with the subject and was too intimidated to ask the teacher for help. The student's need was masked however by her disorganised approach and "cool" attitude. The teacher was unaware of the student's worries and was under the impression that the student wasn't very interested in improving her skills. We adapted the language to suit the situation:

- *How do you feel in this subject?*
- *Who is affected?*
- *What can we do to repair the situation?*

The result was very satisfactory and both the student and the teacher are working together cooperatively. The student's mother was also very happy with the outcome and relieved that the teacher did not see her as a whining parent. In following up some weeks later, the student happily reported, "I understand everything". This is a great result, not only because of the repaired relationship between teacher and student and the student's improved academic performance, but because both participants felt positive about the mini-conferencing process and will be comfortable using it again if needed.

3. Community conferencing in the curriculum: role-play

As part of the Year 8 anti-bullying programme "Dealing with Feelings", I used a community conference role-play in the classroom to show students the impact of bullying across the extended school community.

Students were thrown in at the deep end with little preparation besides a basic scenario to follow. I deliberately chose a student who had been a victim of bullying as the wrongdoer so as to give her an understanding of the wrongdoer's experience. Similarly, I chose a confident, popular student to be a victim so as to give her a look at life from a different perspective.

The students did really well and the class was completely focused on the activity. The conference brought together all that we had examined in the "Dealing with Feelings" programme and reinforced the important role bystanders play in bullying situations (expressed through the supporters of both victim and wrongdoer). Before the conference role-play, students had not considered how bullying affects parents and staff. Students wrote very insightful reflections about the community conference and had learned more in those 30 minutes, than in a week's worth of English lessons!

The following interesting observations were made:

- The wrongdoer instantly started off defensive and underplayed the situation
- The victim's body language showed that she still felt victimised
- Both supporters of the wrongdoer and the victim felt at the end of the conference that they needed to take some responsibility and should have intervened in the incident.
- Role-plays can lead to startling moments of self-reflection and revelation!

The student who played the victim in this role-play was quite upset by the end of the conference. At first it appeared that she needed to be debriefed; she did, but for different reasons. As we briefly discussed people's reactions and experiences, this student publicly apologised to the class. She said that she realised that she had been a bully all her life and now she knew how it felt – awful.

I spent time in a debriefing with this student one to one. She was crying and upset but grateful that she had had this opportunity to "walk in someone else's shoes". She was very eager that everyone in Year 8 should see this, as it was her belief that this was the only way to stop "back-stabbing" in the year level. I suggested that we could show a conference to the year level and the student wanted to help in any way she could. She even volunteered to introduce the concept of conferencing to Year 8's and explain why it was so important to experience the process.

As a result we are now implementing her suggestion. She and I, along with the other students from the original role-play, are developing and rehearsing another community conference role-play to show to the rest of Year 8. The students have improved the scenario and wanted to introduce a father to make the families more balanced. We are also complementing this with some of the *Mind Matters* (a mental health programme) material on bullying and resiliency. We will now try to adapt the devised role play into a lesson guide which will allow all teachers across a variety of Key Learning

Restorative Practices in Schools

Areas the opportunity to access the language and benefits of conferencing in their own classroom. Included in this will be a set of questions for students to form the basis of discussion in classrooms after the role-play:

1. *Do you think this is a fair way to deal with serious incidents of bullying? Why/ Why not?*

2. *How do you think the victims felt? Do you think it was important for them to be able to "voice" their feelings?*

3. *How do you think the wrongdoers felt? Do you think it was important for them to hear the other people's stories?*

4. *Do you think things will change for the wrongdoers and victims as a result of the community conference?*

5. *Do you think conferencing is a good way to sort out problems?*

6. *Did you find this role play educational/informative? Explain your answer.*

7. *Is there anything else you would like to say about community conferencing?*

About the authors

Margaret Thorsborne

Margaret has a long history in education, guidance and counselling. Her passion while employed in education had always been to find better ways to build and rebuild relationships between teachers, students and other members of the school community, to enhance teaching and learning outcomes. She and like-minded colleagues were therefore keen to discover more effective interventions to deal with those sorts of incidents in schools such as bullying, abuse, conflict and violence which did not respond positively to traditional punitive sanctions. She was, therefore, inspired by stories of conferencing, then being used in justice agencies. Always a risk-taker, Margaret convened the first ever school-based conference with a little telephone coaching from a police officer, and has never looked back! She managed a ground breaking pilot of community conferencing in her educational region, and is now consultant to a number of government education departments in Australia and abroad wishing to change the policy, practice and culture of behaviour management in schools. Now a private consultant, she continues to work in schools as well as in private and public sector workplaces, convening conferences for high level conflict and inappropriate behaviour and providing training in conference facilitation for middle and senior management.

David Vinegrad

David is a veteran of working in a diversity of school settings and undertaking a wide range of roles in classroom teaching, student counselling and management. His work experience covers several states of Australia and he is now involved in International Schooling in Japan. His interest in Restorative Justice stemmed from a concern about the use of traditional school-based measures when wrongdoing occurred. Student behaviour did not change, much conflict remained unresolved and the chance to promote positive teacher–student relationships was often lost. David was greatly encouraged when he undertook some professional development in Restorative Justice and has since become an innovative leader in classroom approaches. After doing some pioneering work in Tasmania with like-minded educators and police he moved to Victoria to continue spreading the word. At the time of writing David is working 'restoratively' in classrooms with his students as well as acting as consultant to the Ministry of Education Singapore and a number of International schools in Japan.

Other titles on Restorative Practices by
Margaret Thorsborne & David Vinegrad

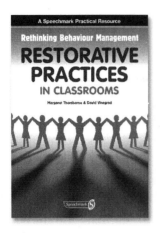

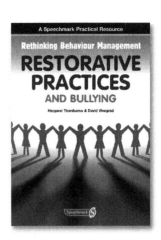

Restorative Practices in Classrooms

Focusing specifically on the classroom, this essential title includes

- How to analyse the current classrooms practice

- How to use the 'Community Conference' process to minimise the risk of classroom disruption

- Step-by-step instructions for preparation, planning and facilitation of individual, small group, large group and whole classroom conferences

- Key master documents that can be adapted.

Restorative Practices and Bullying

The authors offer a useful guide to dealing with this difficult subject:

- Restorative justice and behaviour management

- An explanation of the restorative practice approach to bullying

- Detailed descriptions of restorative responses to bullying incidents

- Frequently asked questions and answers

- Case studies.